MUD, MUD, GLORIOUS MUD...

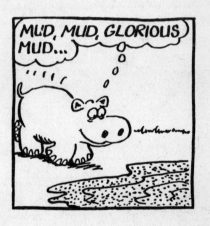

Also available from Warner Books

CREATURE FEATURE VOLUME 1

CREATURE FEATURE
2

...BY DAVE FOLLOWS.

WARNER BOOKS

A *Warner* Book

First published in Great Britain
by Warner Books in 1994

Copyright © Dave Follows & Advance Features 1994

The moral right of the author has been asserted.

A CIP catalogue record for this book
is available from the British Library.

ISBN 0 7515 0773 3

Printed in England by Clays Ltd, St Ives plc

Warner Books
A Division of
Little, Brown and Company (UK) Limited
Brettenham House
Lancaster Place
London WC2E 7EN

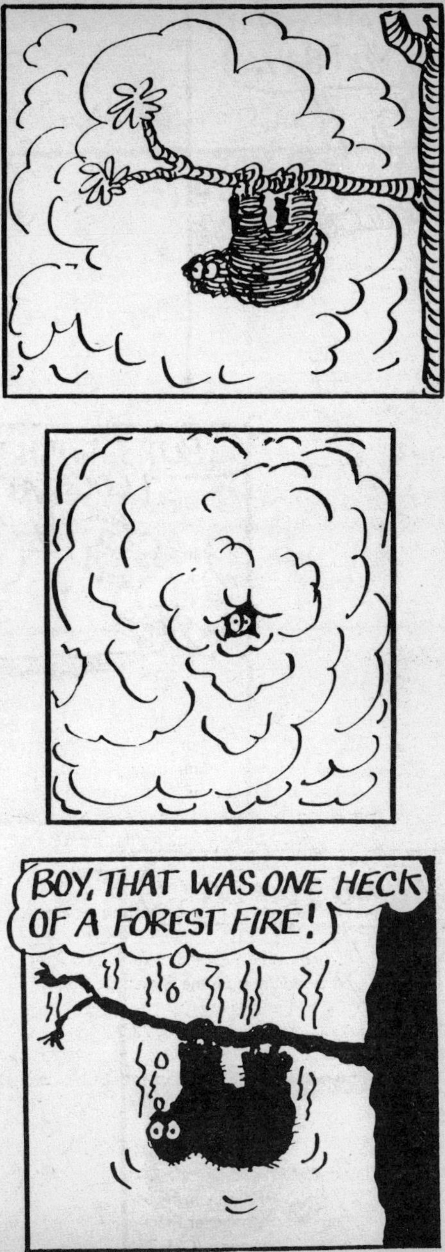
BOY, THAT WAS ONE HECK OF A FOREST FIRE!

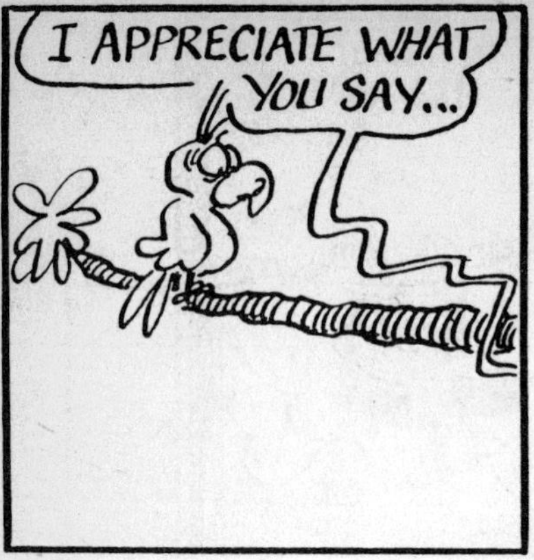
I APPRECIATE WHAT YOU SAY...

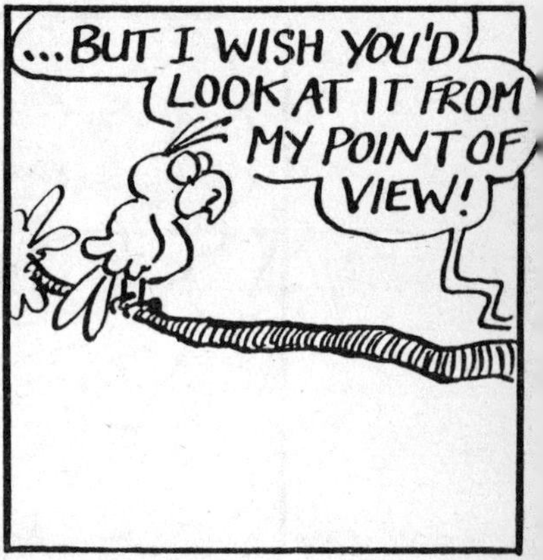
...BUT I WISH YOU'D LOOK AT IT FROM MY POINT OF VIEW!

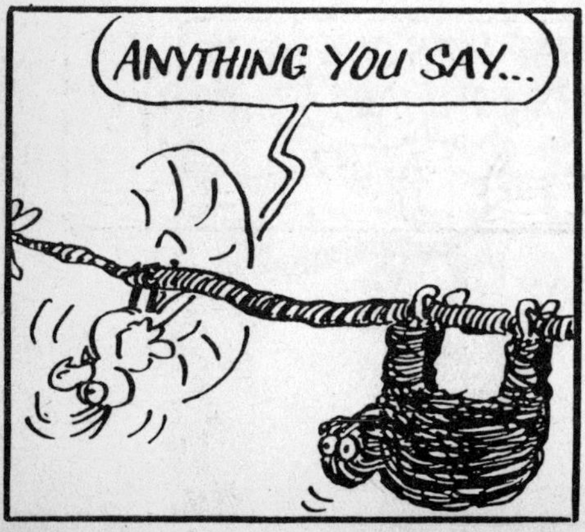
ANYTHING YOU SAY...

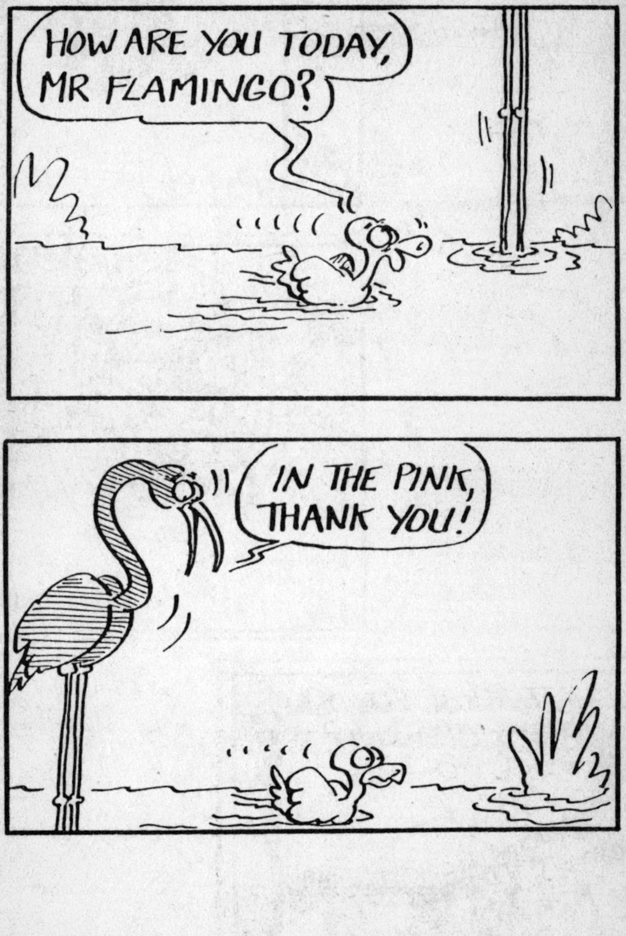
HOW ARE YOU TODAY, MR FLAMINGO?
IN THE PINK, THANK YOU!

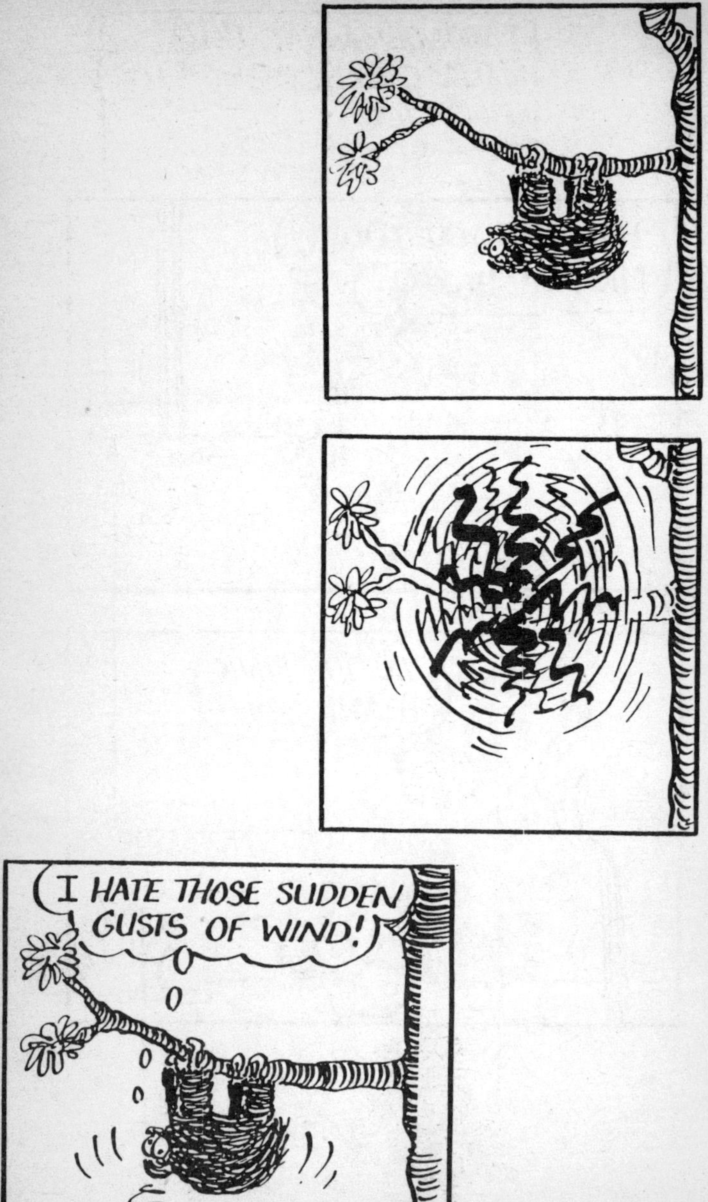
I HATE THOSE SUDDEN GUSTS OF WIND!

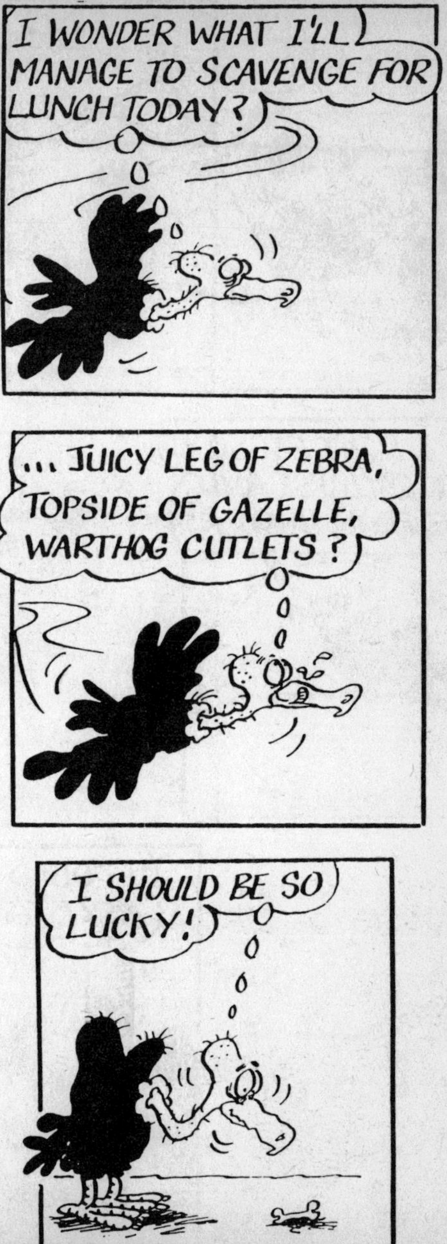
I WONDER WHAT I'LL MANAGE TO SCAVENGE FOR LUNCH TODAY?
... JUICY LEG OF ZEBRA, TOPSIDE OF GAZELLE, WARTHOG CUTLETS?
I SHOULD BE SO LUCKY!

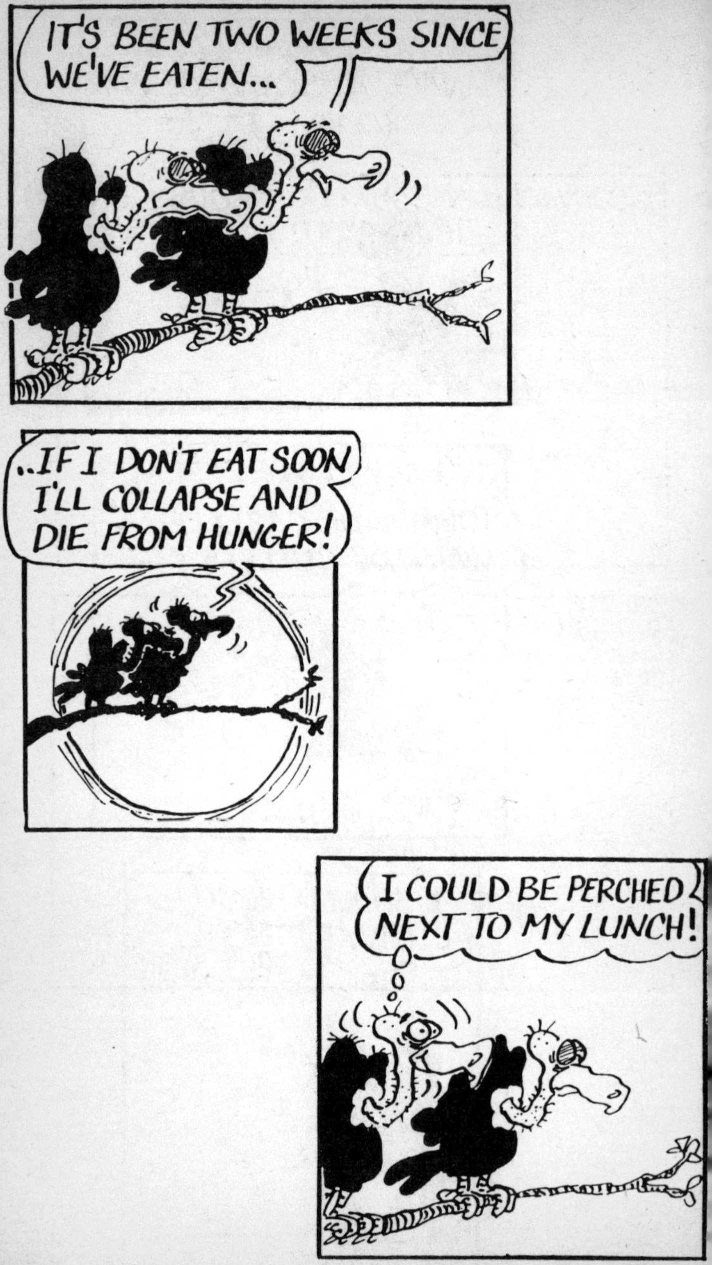
IT'S BEEN TWO WEEKS SINCE WE'VE EATEN...
..IF I DON'T EAT SOON I'LL COLLAPSE AND DIE FROM HUNGER!
I COULD BE PERCHED NEXT TO MY LUNCH!

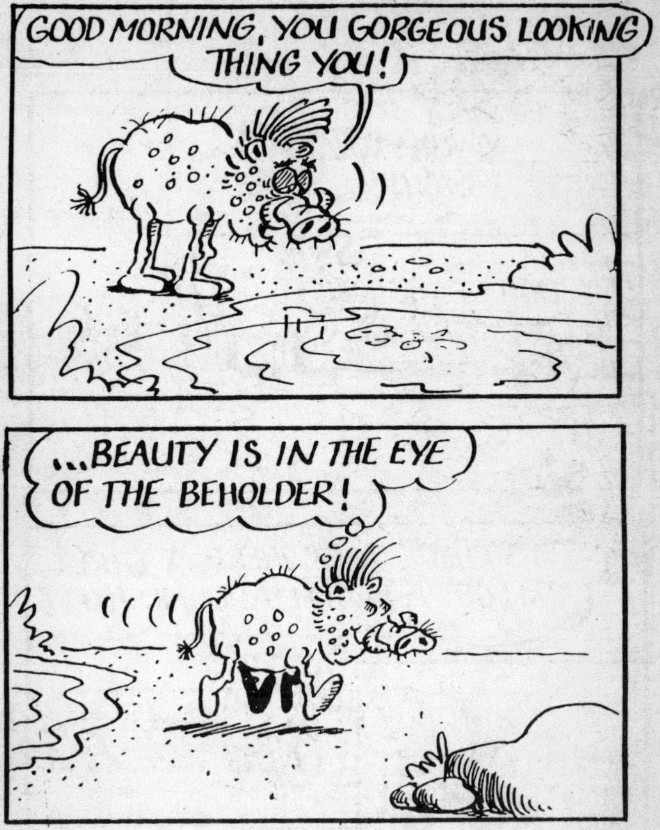
GOOD MORNING, YOU GORGEOUS LOOKING THING YOU!
...BEAUTY IS IN THE EYE OF THE BEHOLDER!

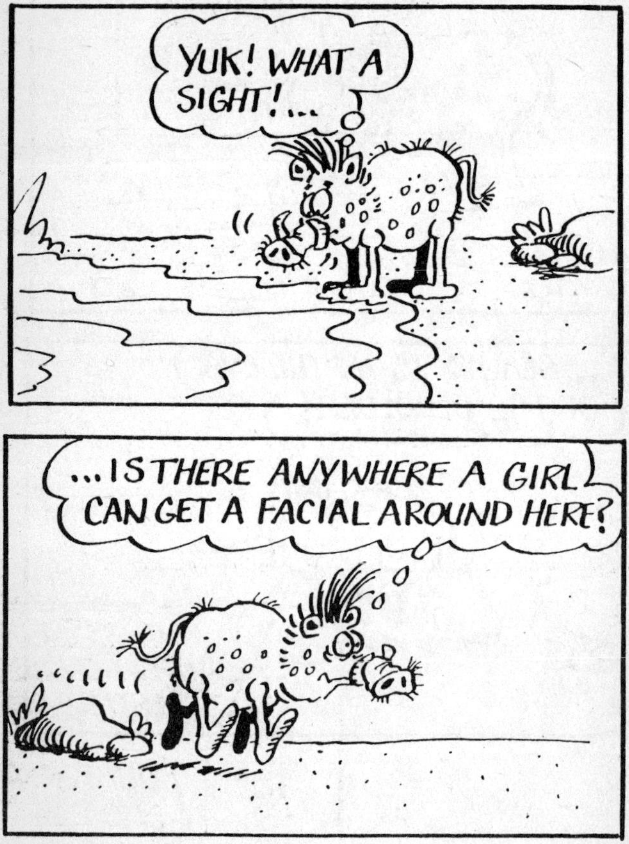
YUK! WHAT A SIGHT!...
...IS THERE ANYWHERE A GIRL CAN GET A FACIAL AROUND HERE?

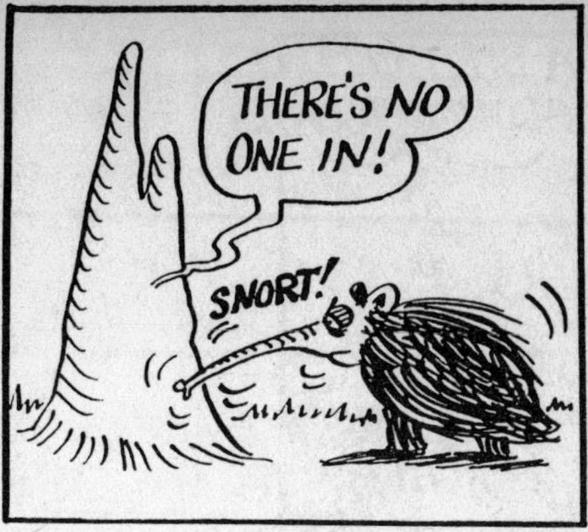
THERE'S NO ONE IN!
SNORT!

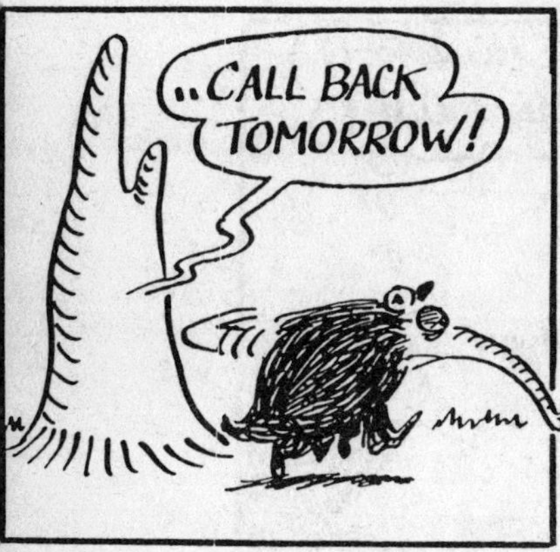
..CALL BACK TOMORROW!

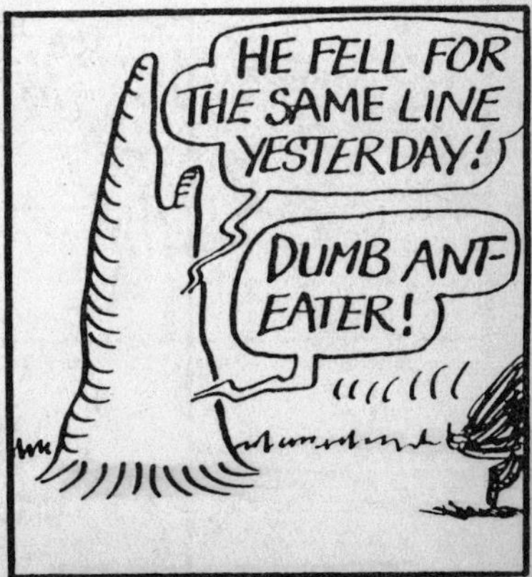
HE FELL FOR THE SAME LINE YESTERDAY!
DUMB ANT-EATER!

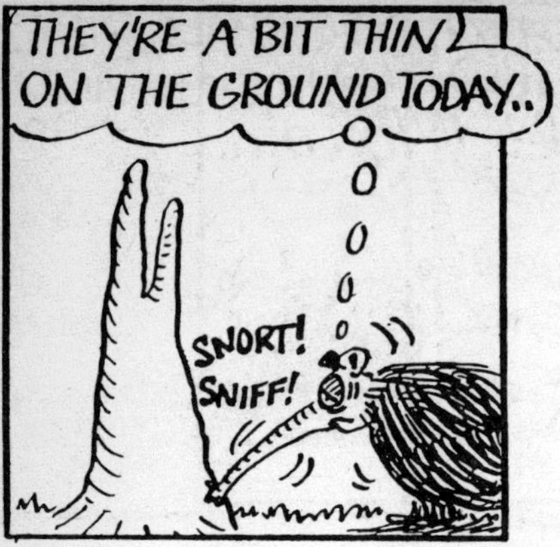
THEY'RE A BIT THIN ON THE GROUND TODAY..
SNORT!
SNIFF!

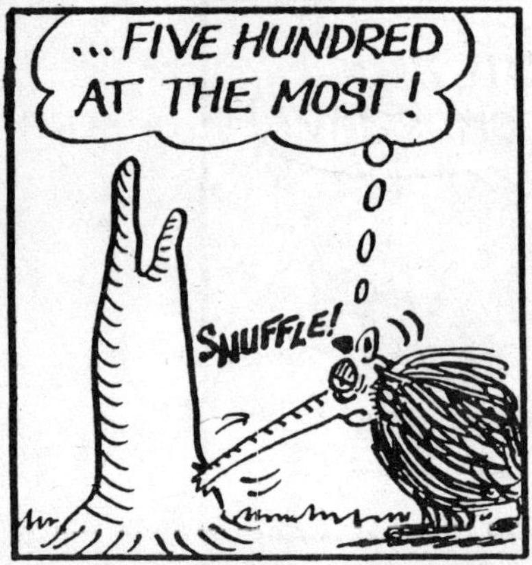
...FIVE HUNDRED AT THE MOST!
SNUFFLE!

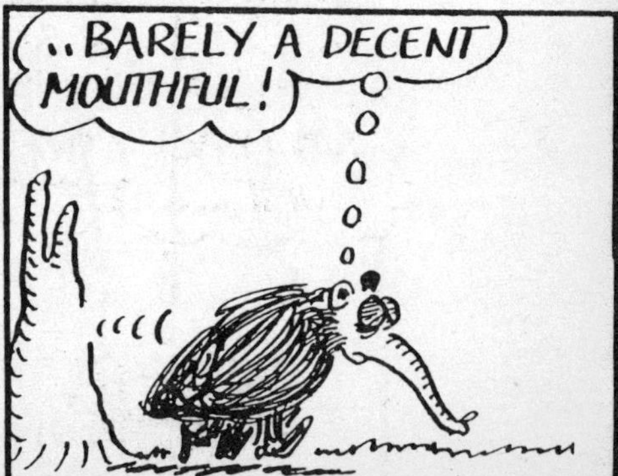
..BARELY A DECENT MOUTHFUL!

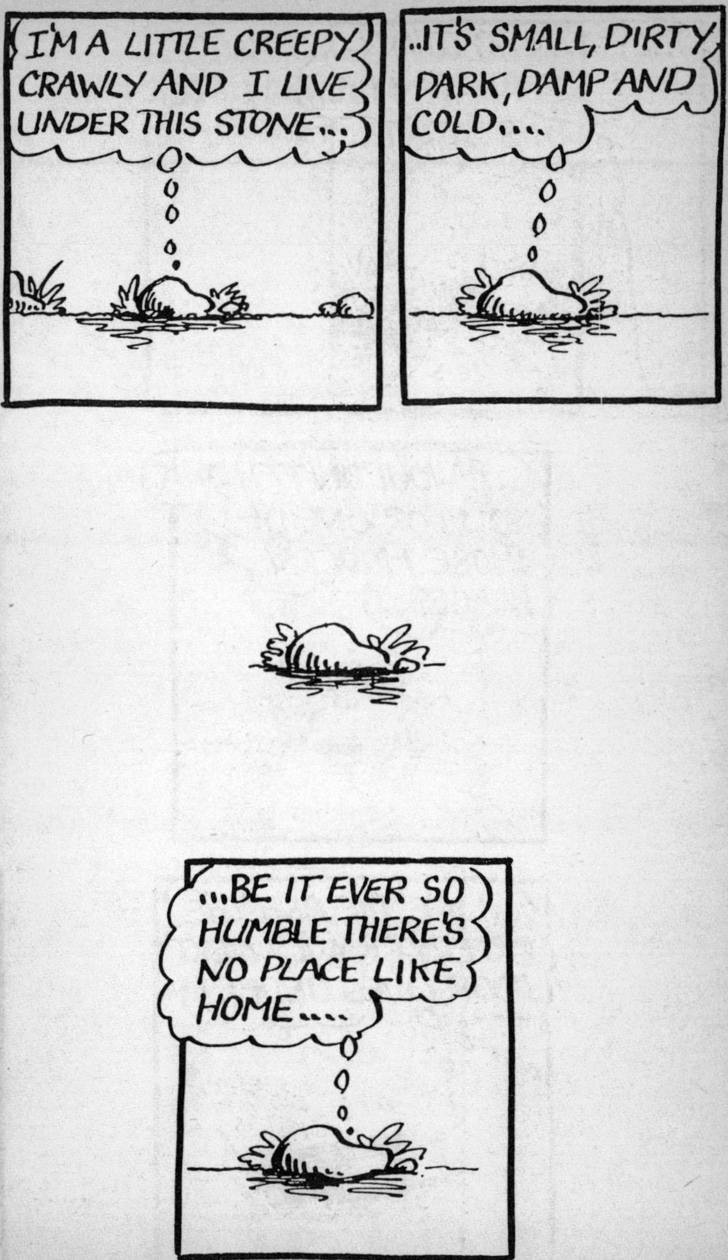
I'M A LITTLE CREEPY CRAWLY AND I LIVE UNDER THIS STONE...
..IT'S SMALL, DIRTY, DARK, DAMP AND COLD....
...BE IT EVER SO HUMBLE THERE'S NO PLACE LIKE HOME....

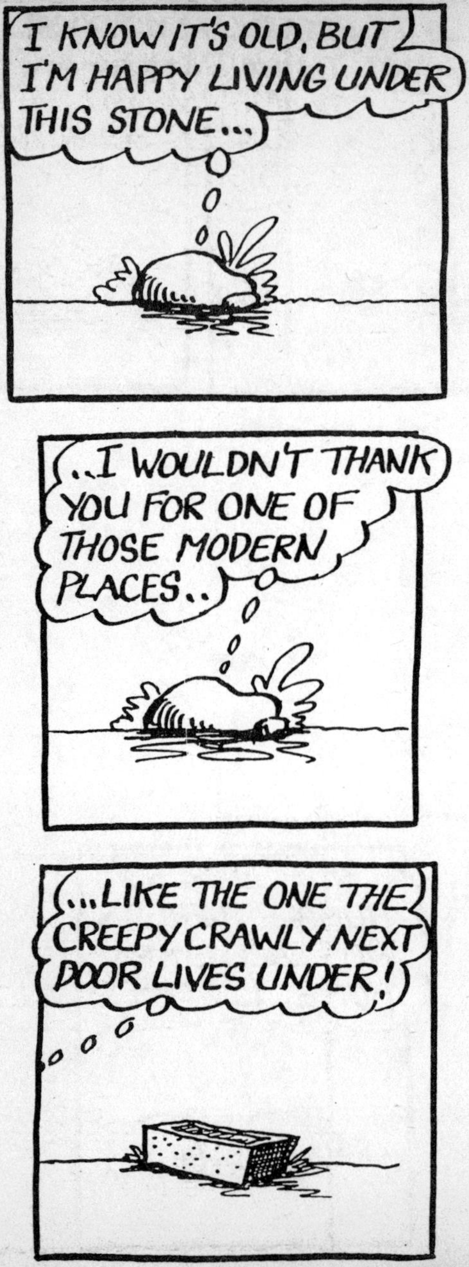
I KNOW IT'S OLD, BUT I'M HAPPY LIVING UNDER THIS STONE...
...I WOULDN'T THANK YOU FOR ONE OF THOSE MODERN PLACES..
...LIKE THE ONE THE CREEPY CRAWLY NEXT DOOR LIVES UNDER!

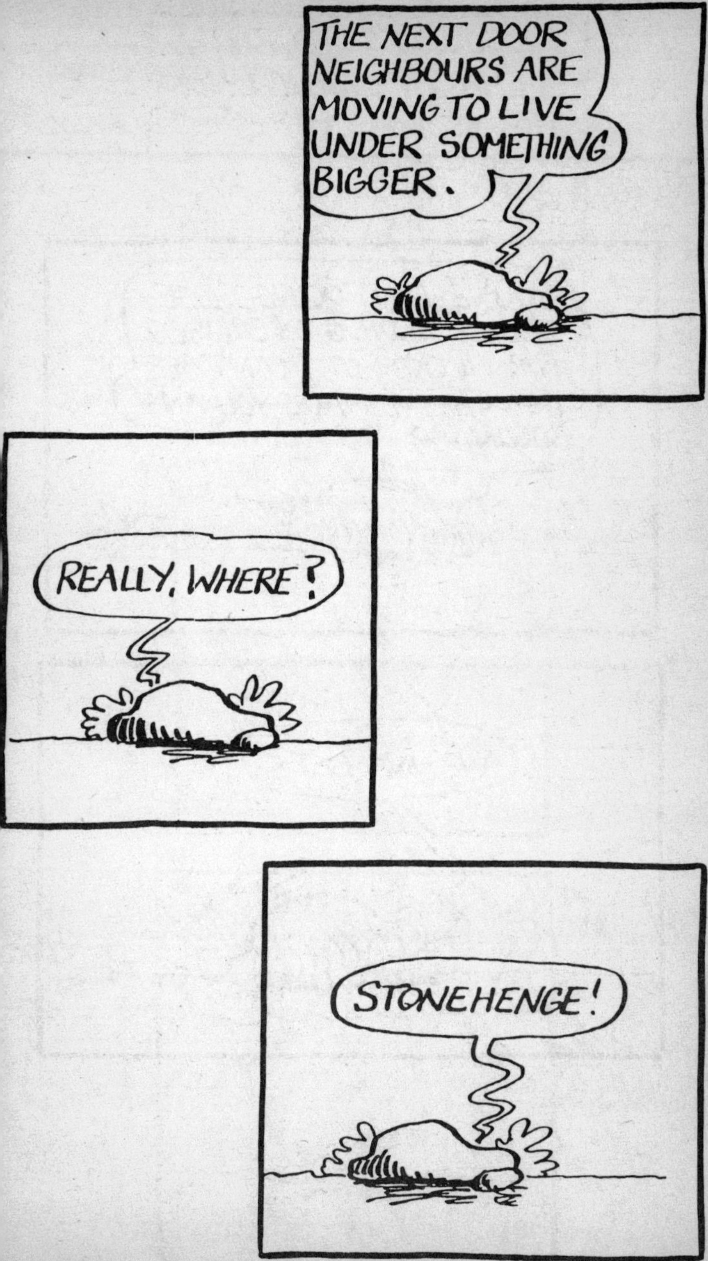
THE NEXT DOOR NEIGHBOURS ARE MOVING TO LIVE UNDER SOMETHING BIGGER.
REALLY, WHERE?
STONEHENGE!

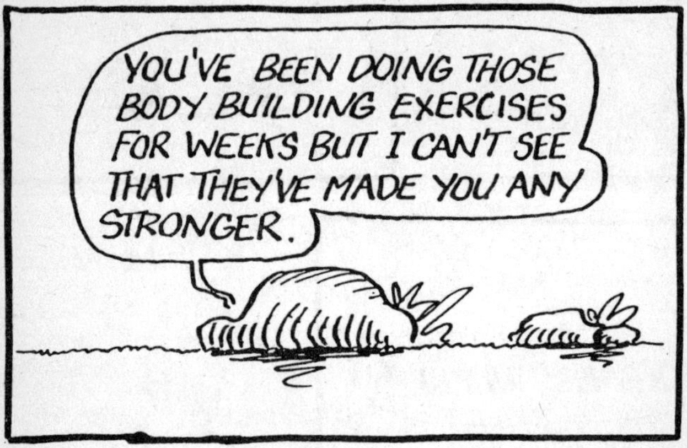
YOU'VE BEEN DOING THOSE BODY BUILDING EXERCISES FOR WEEKS BUT I CAN'T SEE THAT THEY'VE MADE YOU ANY STRONGER.

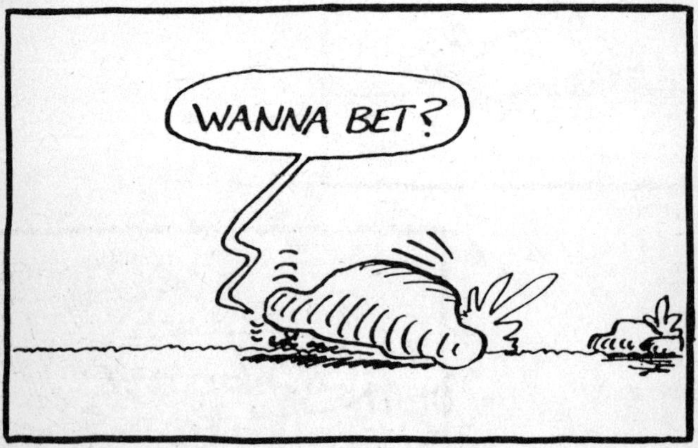
WANNA BET?

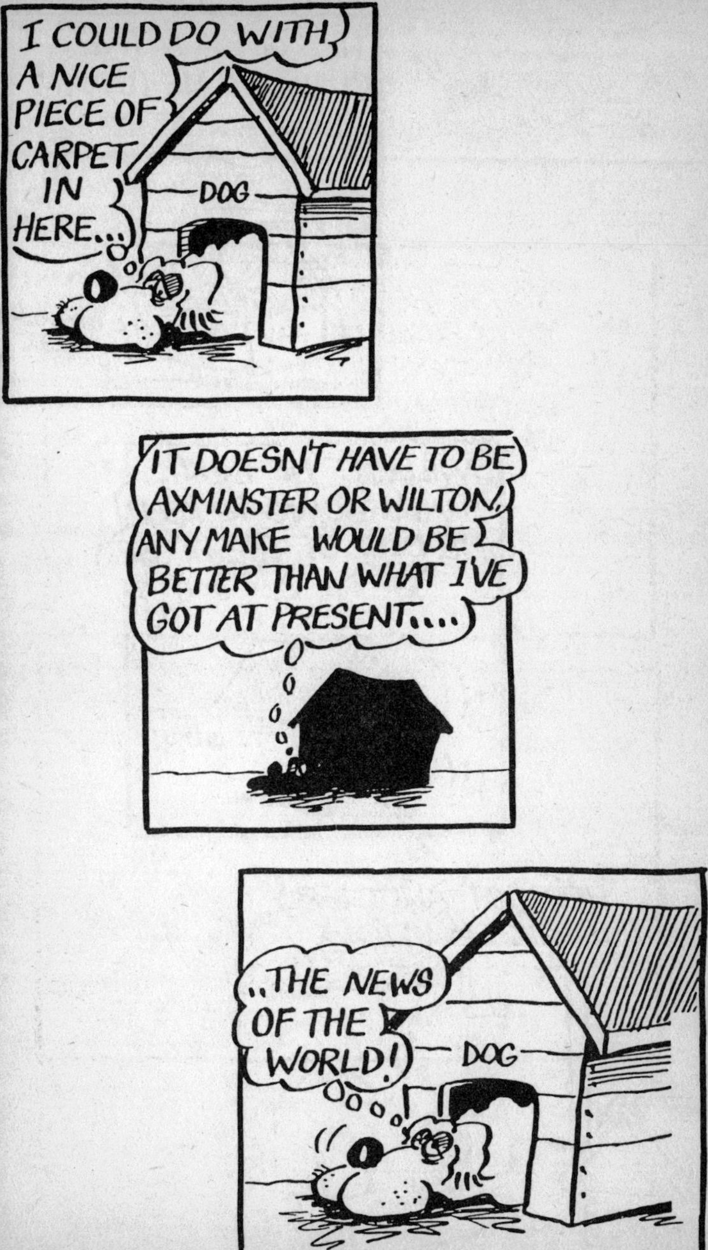
I COULD DO WITH A NICE PIECE OF CARPET IN HERE...
DOG
IT DOESN'T HAVE TO BE AXMINSTER OR WILTON, ANY MAKE WOULD BE BETTER THAN WHAT I'VE GOT AT PRESENT....
..THE NEWS OF THE WORLD!
DOG

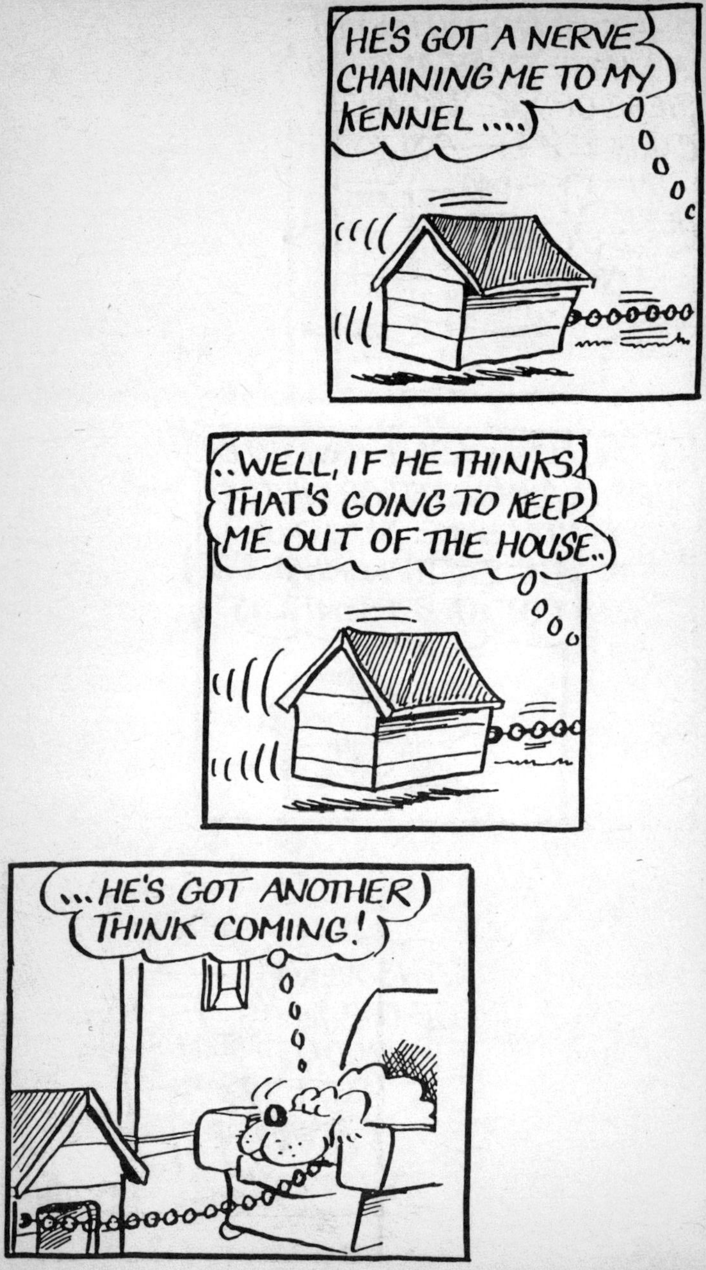
HE'S GOT A NERVE CHAINING ME TO MY KENNEL....
..WELL, IF HE THINKS THAT'S GOING TO KEEP ME OUT OF THE HOUSE..
...HE'S GOT ANOTHER THINK COMING!

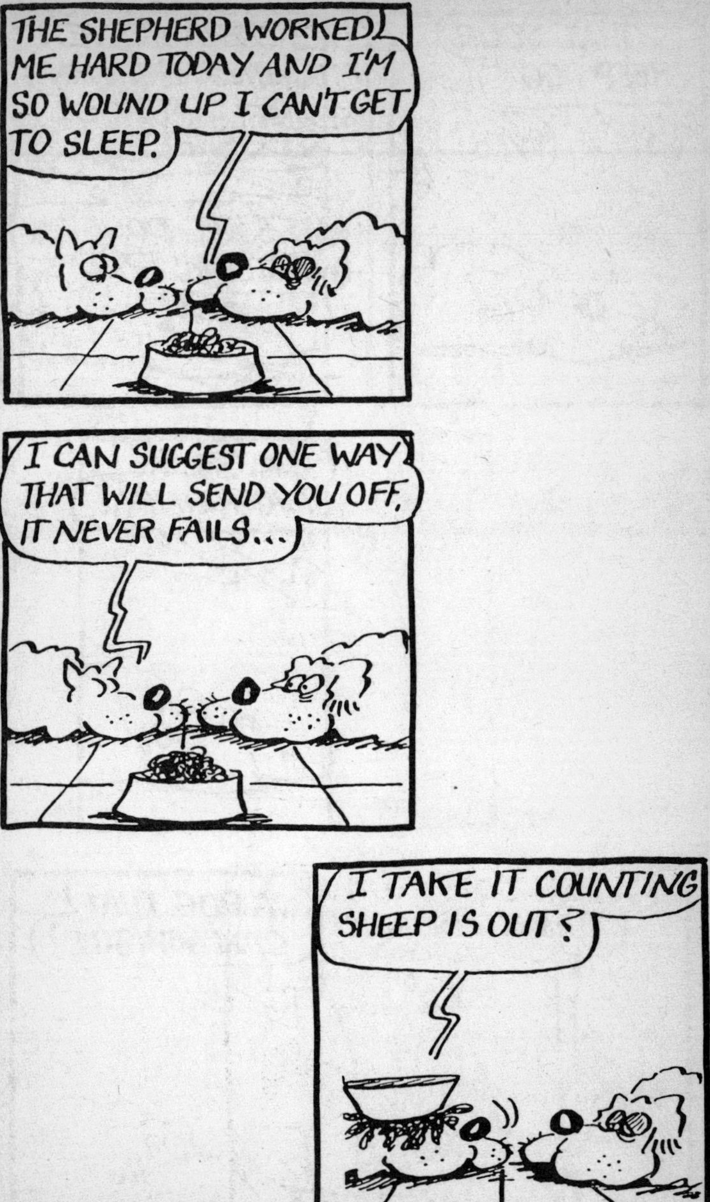
THE SHEPHERD WORKED ME HARD TODAY AND I'M SO WOUND UP I CAN'T GET TO SLEEP.
I CAN SUGGEST ONE WAY THAT WILL SEND YOU OFF, IT NEVER FAILS...
I TAKE IT COUNTING SHEEP IS OUT?

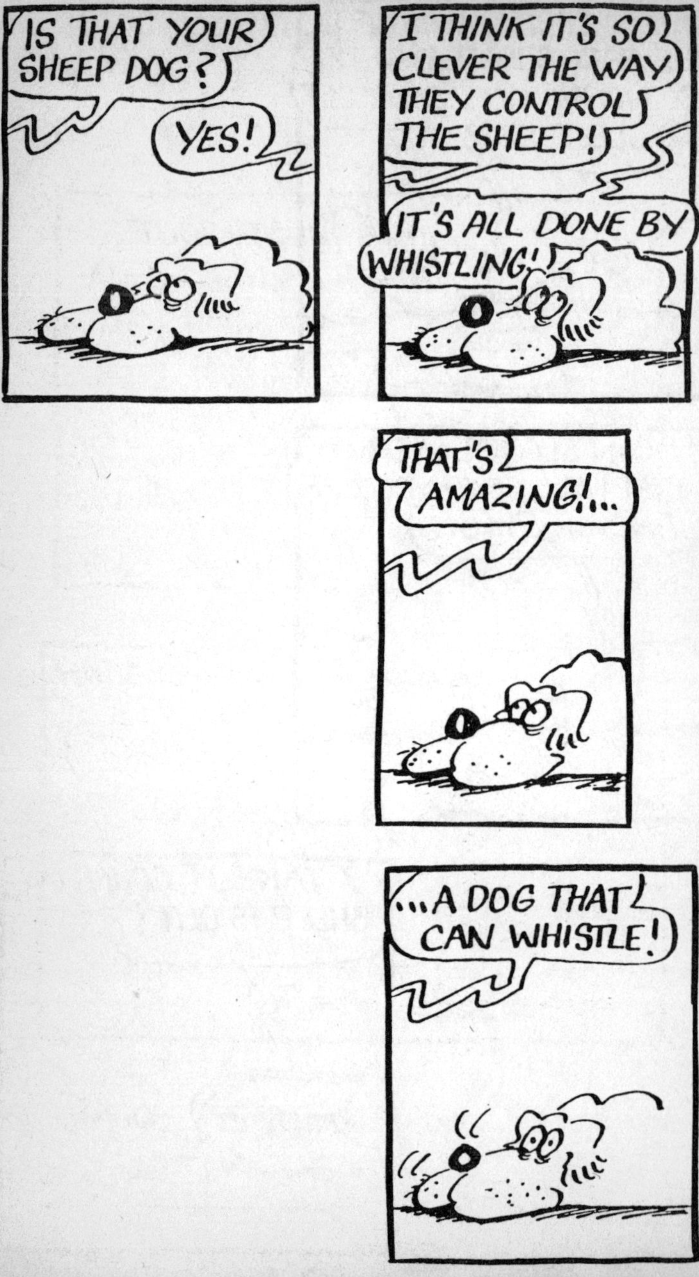
IS THAT YOUR SHEEP DOG?
YES!
I THINK IT'S SO CLEVER THE WAY THEY CONTROL THE SHEEP!
IT'S ALL DONE BY WHISTLING!
THAT'S AMAZING!...
...A DOG THAT CAN WHISTLE!

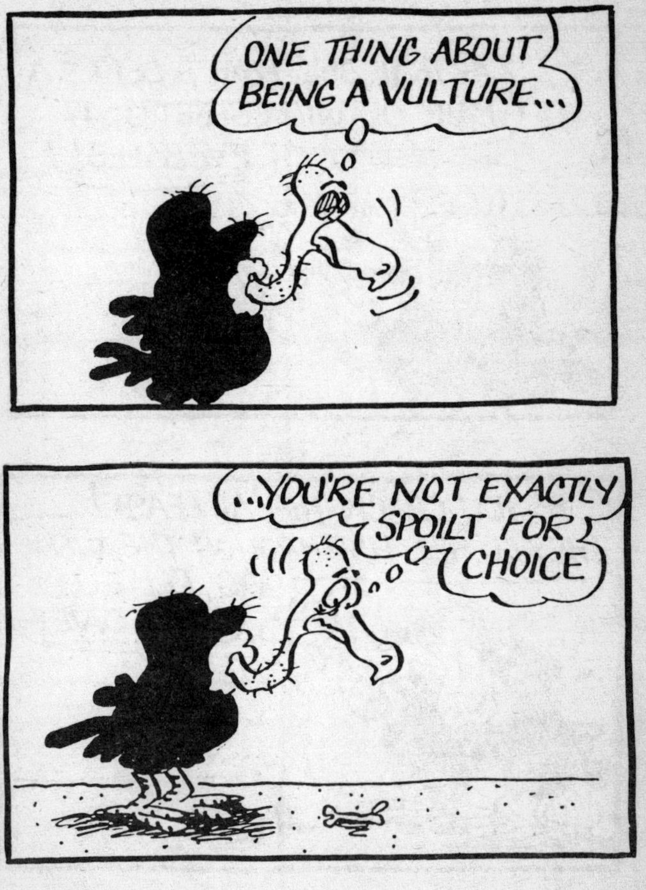
ONE THING ABOUT BEING A VULTURE...
...YOU'RE NOT EXACTLY SPOILT FOR CHOICE

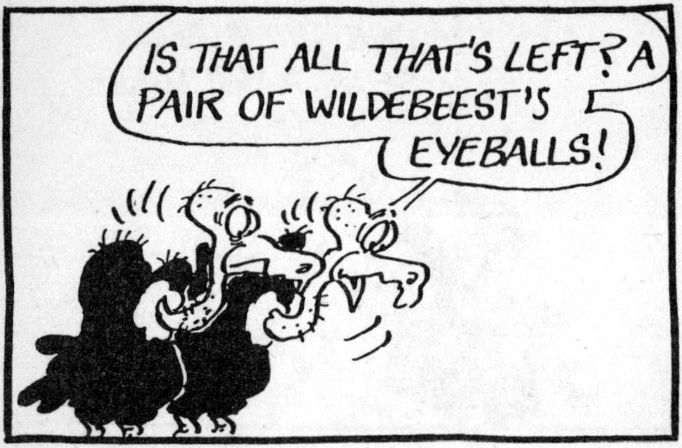
IS THAT ALL THAT'S LEFT? A PAIR OF WILDEBEEST'S EYEBALLS!

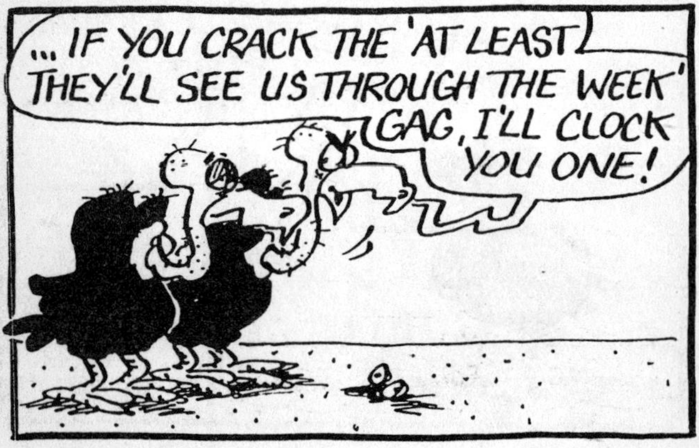
... IF YOU CRACK THE 'AT LEAST THEY'LL SEE US THROUGH THE WEEK' GAG, I'LL CLOCK YOU ONE!

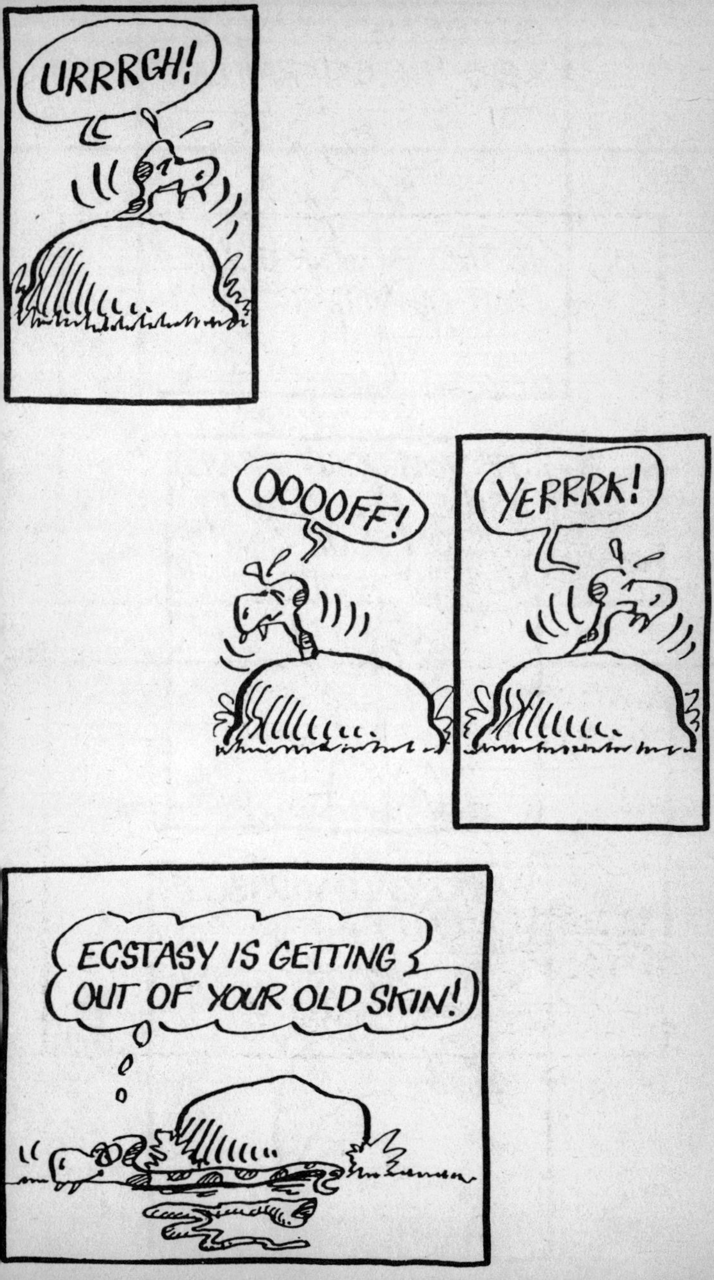
URRRGH!
OOOOFF!
YERRRK!
ECSTASY IS GETTING OUT OF YOUR OLD SKIN!

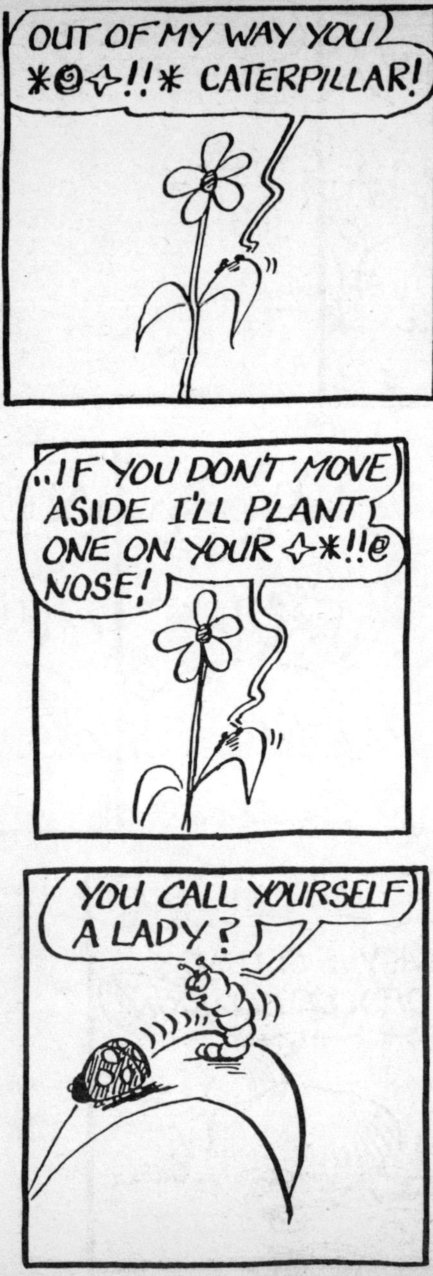
OUT OF MY WAY YOU *@✧!!* CATERPILLAR!
..IF YOU DON'T MOVE ASIDE I'LL PLANT ONE ON YOUR ✧*!!@ NOSE!
YOU CALL YOURSELF A LADY?

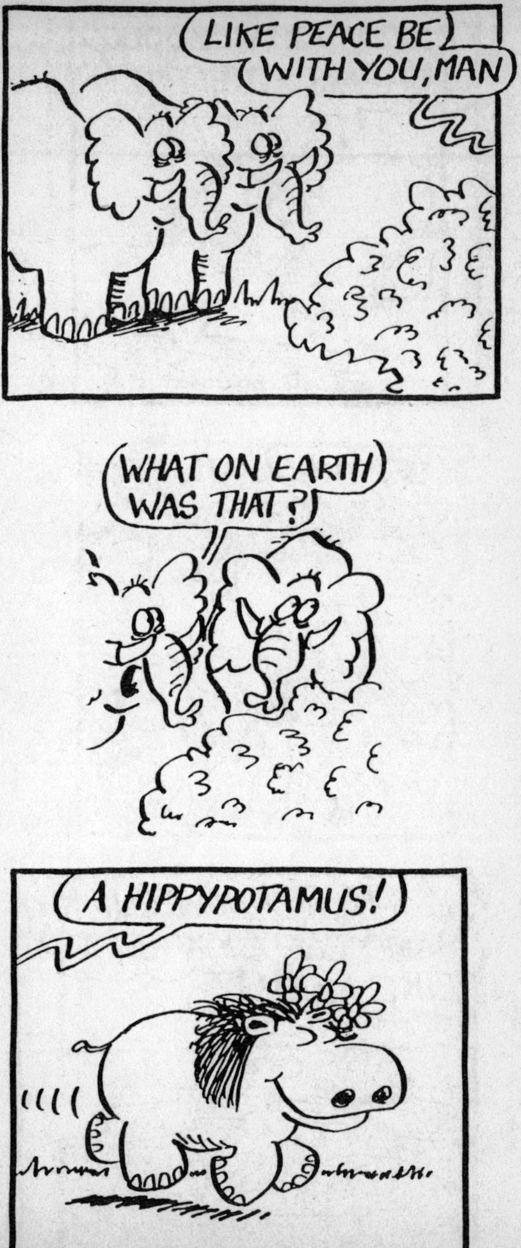
LIKE PEACE BE WITH YOU, MAN
WHAT ON EARTH WAS THAT?
A HIPPYPOTAMUS!

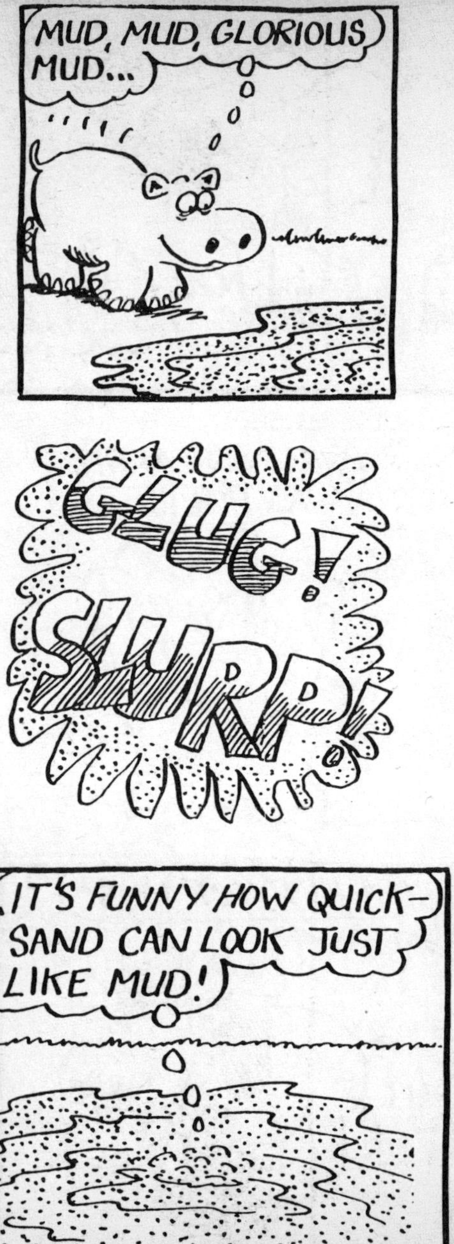
MUD, MUD, GLORIOUS MUD...
GLUG!
SLURP!
..IT'S FUNNY HOW QUICK-SAND CAN LOOK JUST LIKE MUD!

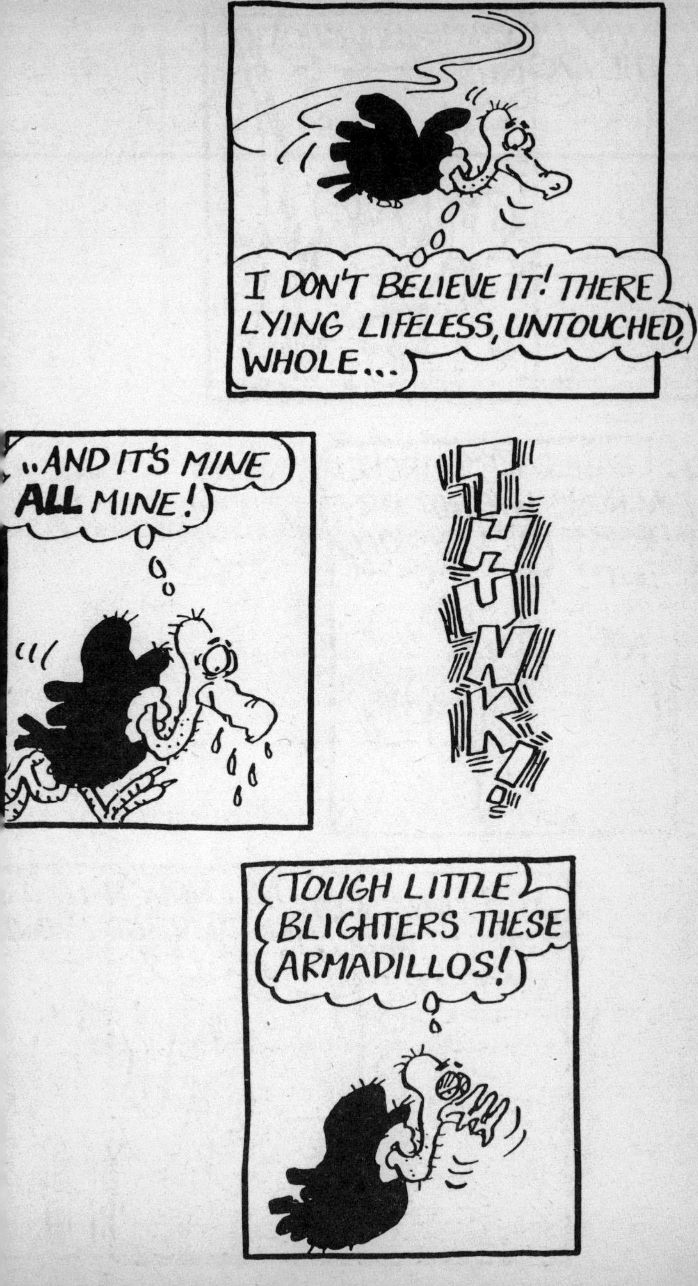
I DON'T BELIEVE IT! THERE LYING LIFELESS, UNTOUCHED, WHOLE...
..AND IT'S MINE ALL MINE!
THUNK!
TOUGH LITTLE BLIGHTERS THESE ARMADILLOS!

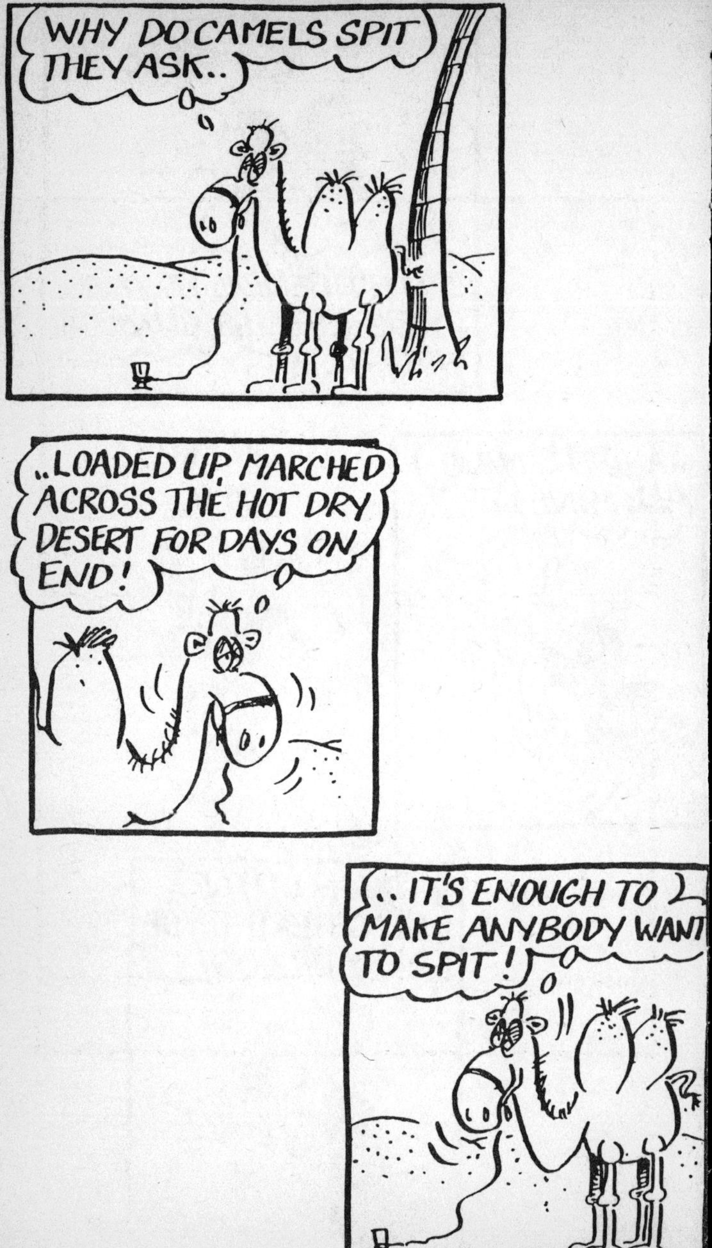
WHY DO CAMELS SPIT THEY ASK..
..LOADED UP, MARCHED ACROSS THE HOT DRY DESERT FOR DAYS ON END!
.. IT'S ENOUGH TO MAKE ANYBODY WANT TO SPIT!

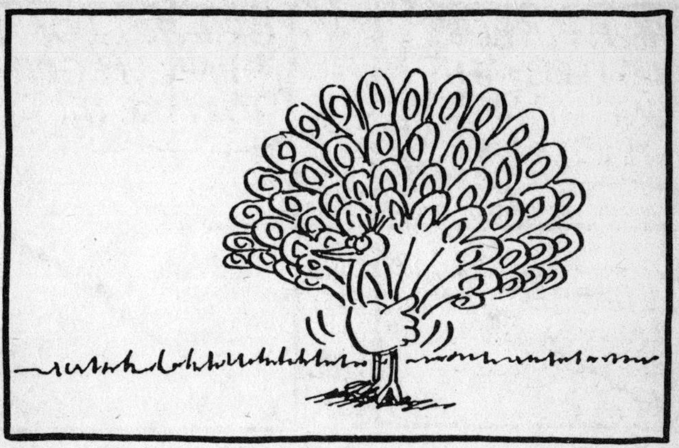

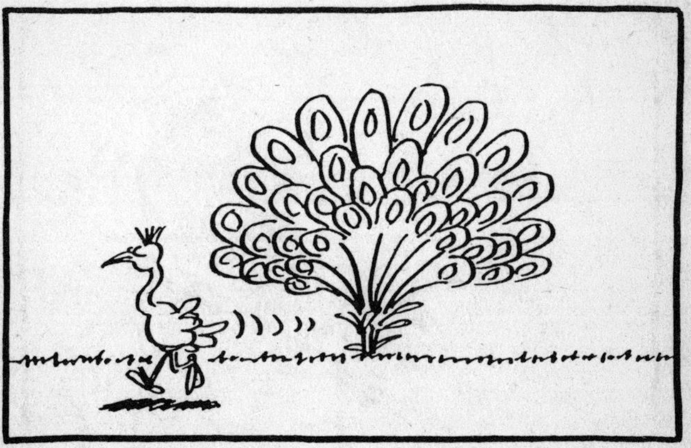

PHEW! PUSHING THIS ELEPHANT DUNG UP HERE IS HARD WORK
GRUNT! I DON'T THINK I'M GOING TO MAKE IT!

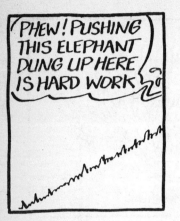

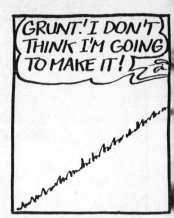

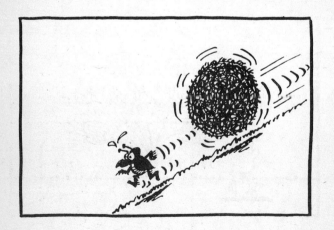

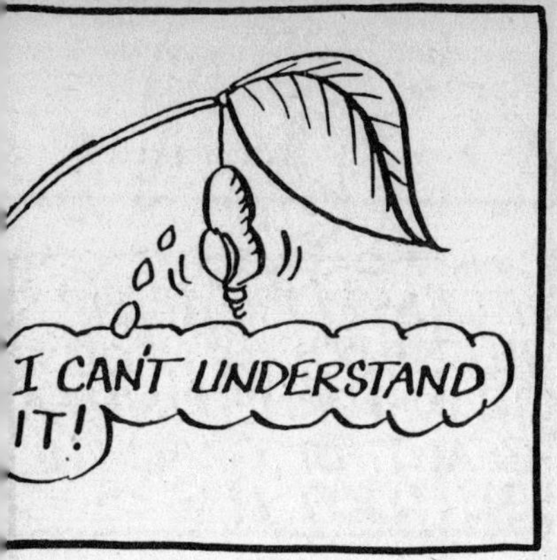
I CAN'T UNDERSTAND IT!

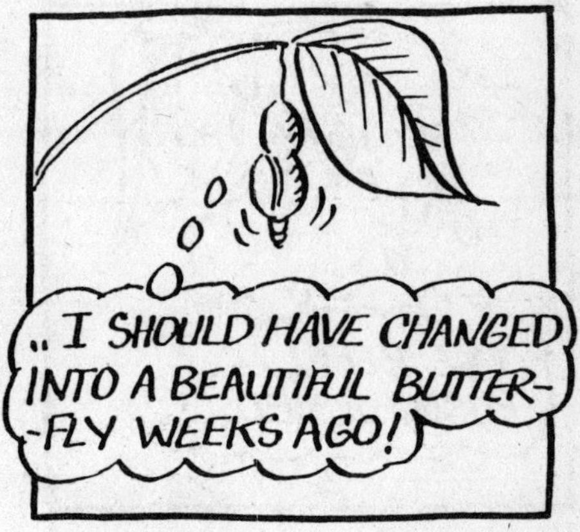
.. I SHOULD HAVE CHANGED INTO A BEAUTIFUL BUTTER--FLY WEEKS AGO!

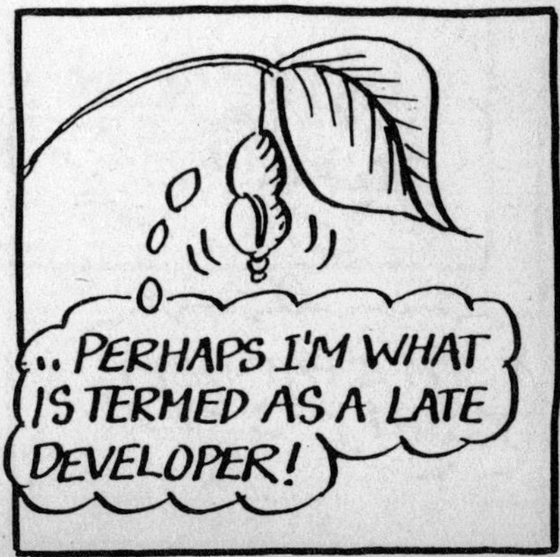
.. PERHAPS I'M WHAT IS TERMED AS A LATE DEVELOPER!

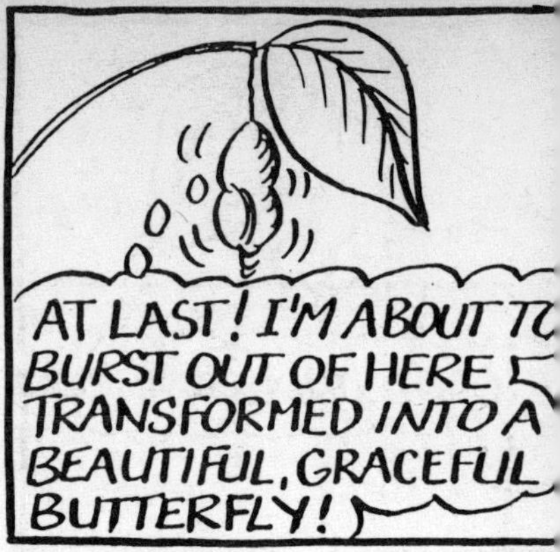
AT LAST! I'M ABOUT TO BURST OUT OF HERE TRANSFORMED INTO A BEAUTIFUL, GRACEFUL BUTTERFLY!

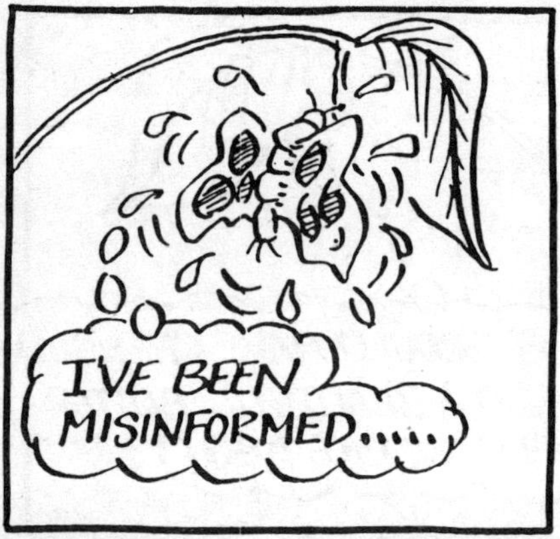
I'VE BEEN MISINFORMED.....

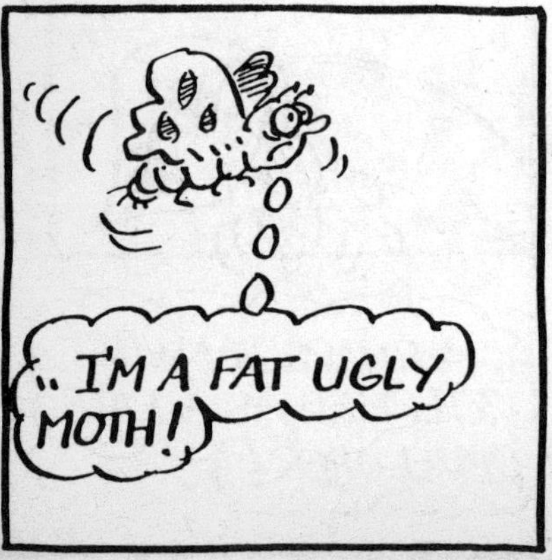
.. I'M A FAT UGLY MOTH!

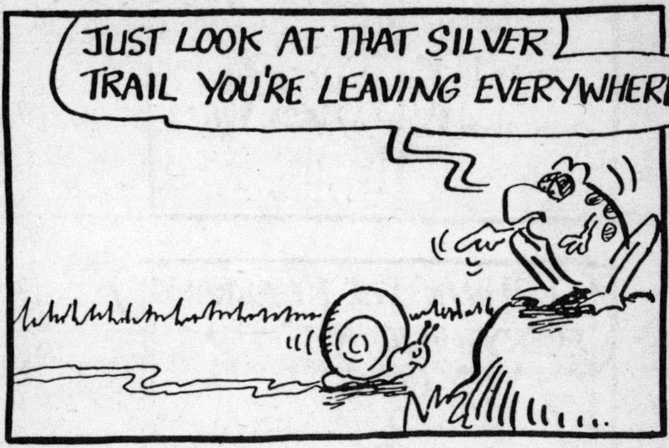
JUST LOOK AT THAT SILVER TRAIL YOU'RE LEAVING EVERYWHERE!

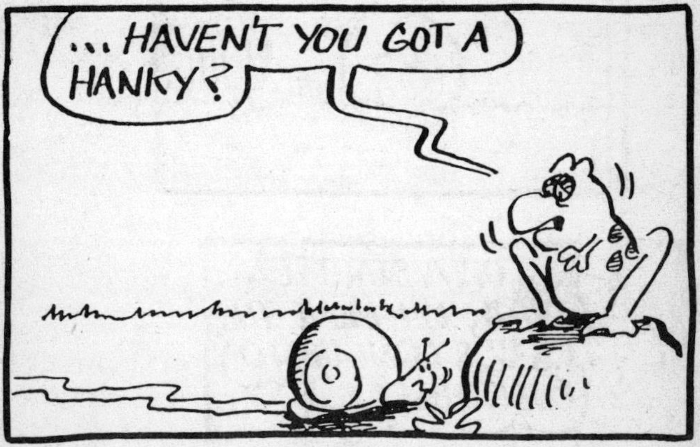
...HAVEN'T YOU GOT A HANKY?

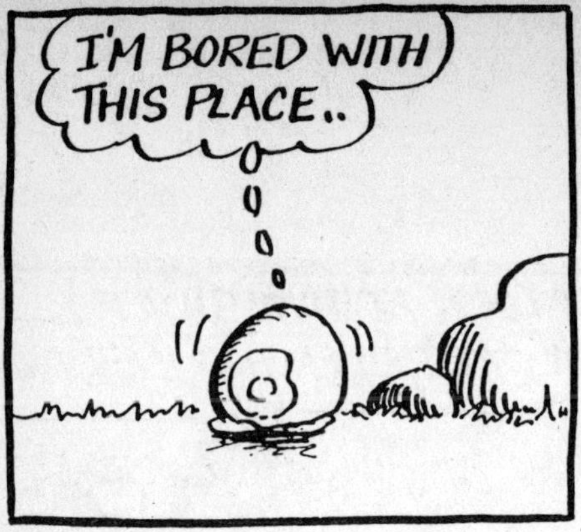
I'M BORED WITH THIS PLACE..

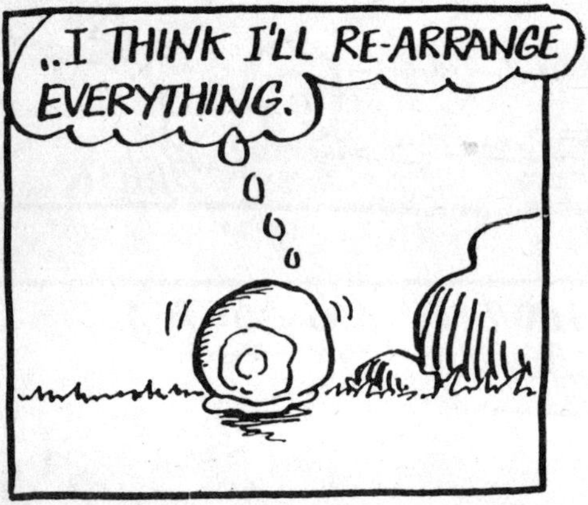
..I THINK I'LL RE-ARRANGE EVERYTHING.

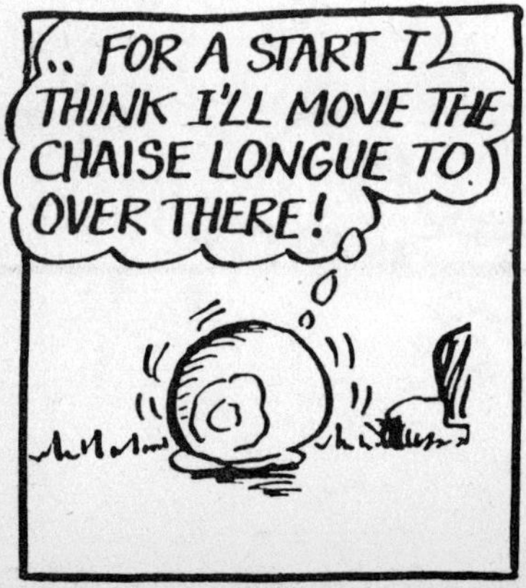
.. FOR A START I THINK I'LL MOVE THE CHAISE LONGUE TO OVER THERE!

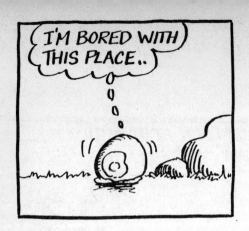

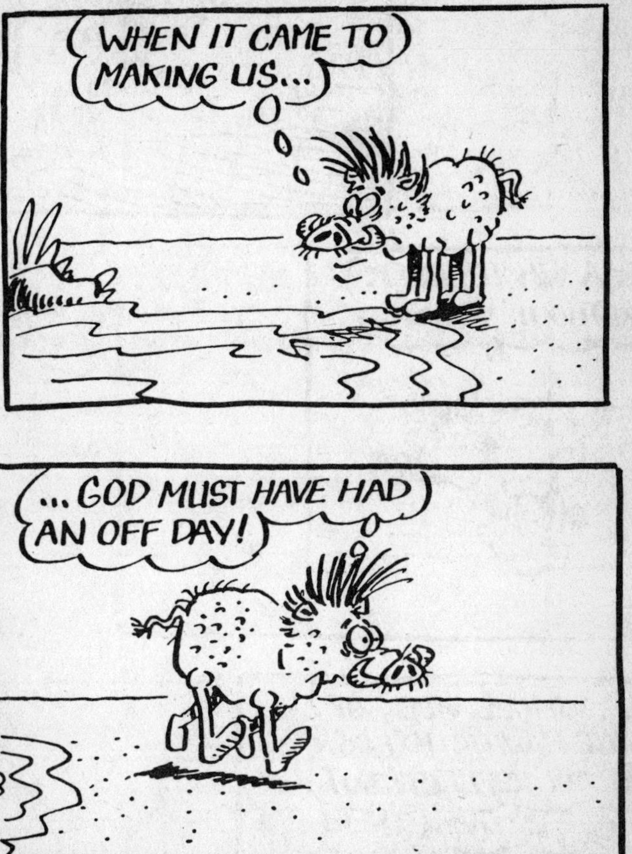
WHEN IT CAME TO MAKING US...
...GOD MUST HAVE HAD AN OFF DAY!

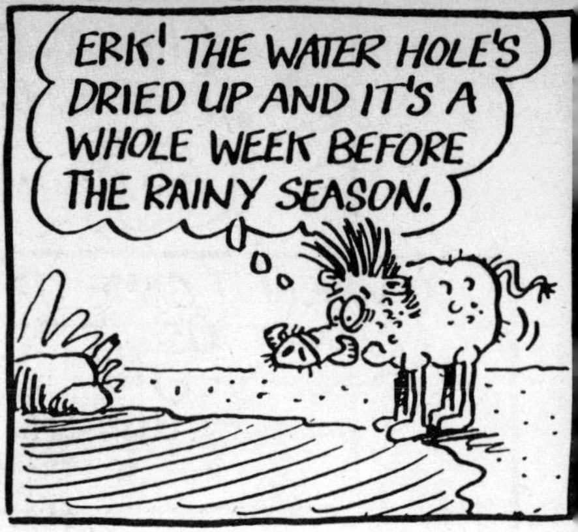
ERK! THE WATER HOLE'S DRIED UP AND IT'S A WHOLE WEEK BEFORE THE RAINY SEASON.

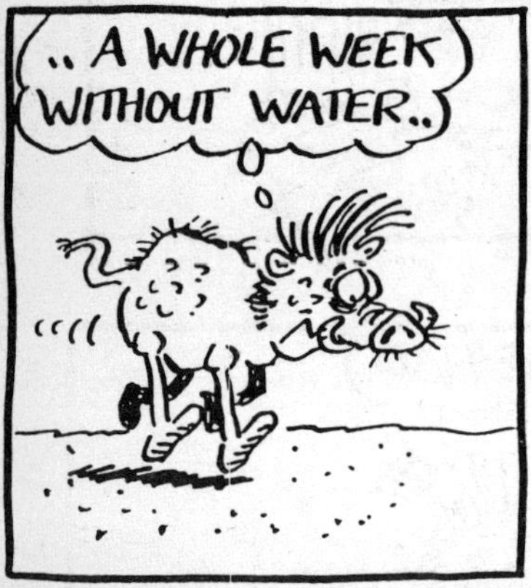
.. A WHOLE WEEK WITHOUT WATER..

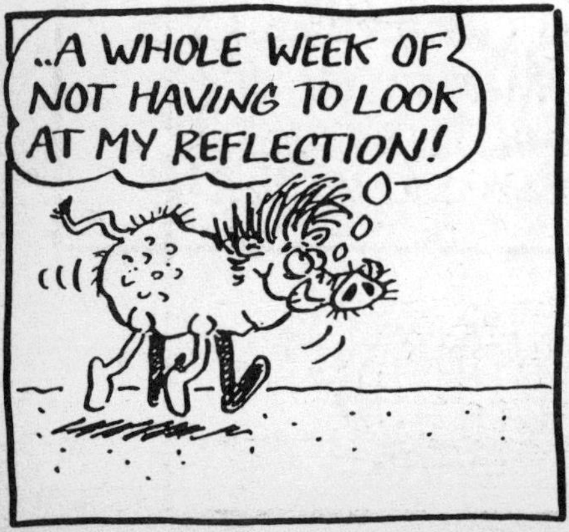
..A WHOLE WEEK OF NOT HAVING TO LOOK AT MY REFLECTION!

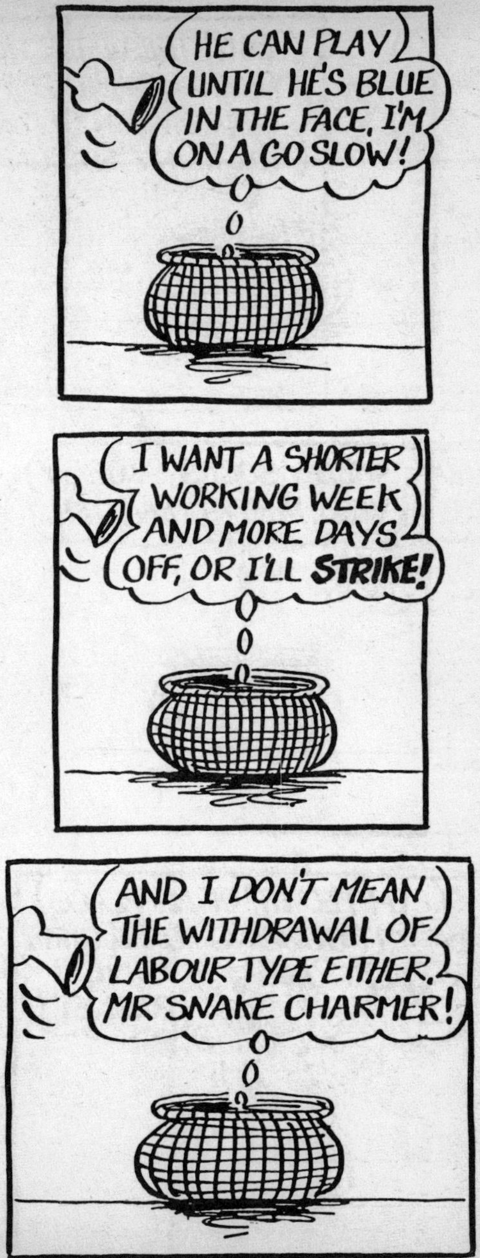
HE CAN PLAY UNTIL HE'S BLUE IN THE FACE, I'M ON A GO SLOW!
I WANT A SHORTER WORKING WEEK AND MORE DAYS OFF, OR I'LL **STRIKE!**
AND I DON'T MEAN THE WITHDRAWAL OF LABOUR TYPE EITHER, MR SNAKE CHARMER!

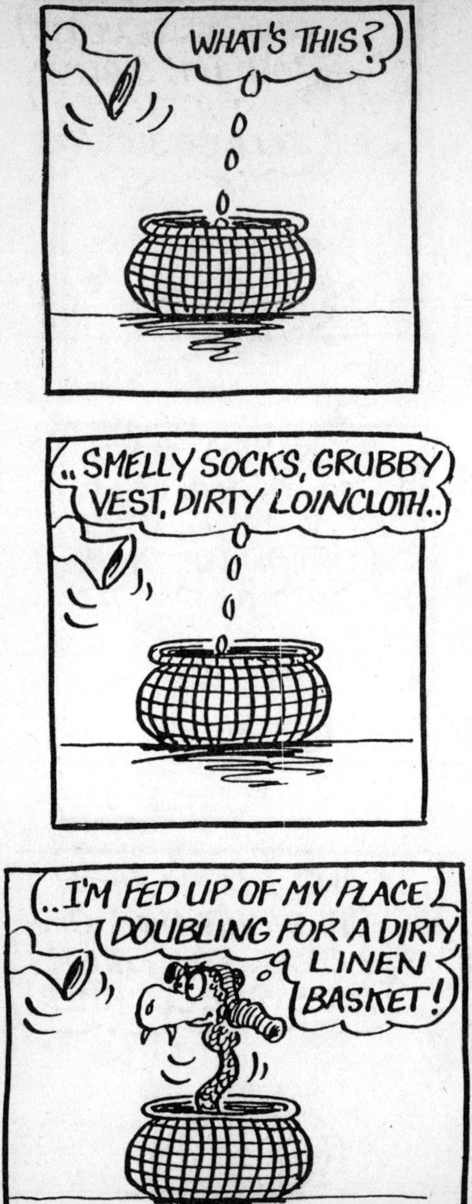
WHAT'S THIS?
.. SMELLY SOCKS, GRUBBY VEST, DIRTY LOINCLOTH..
.. I'M FED UP OF MY PLACE DOUBLING FOR A DIRTY LINEN BASKET!

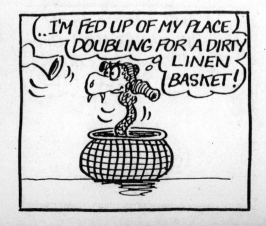

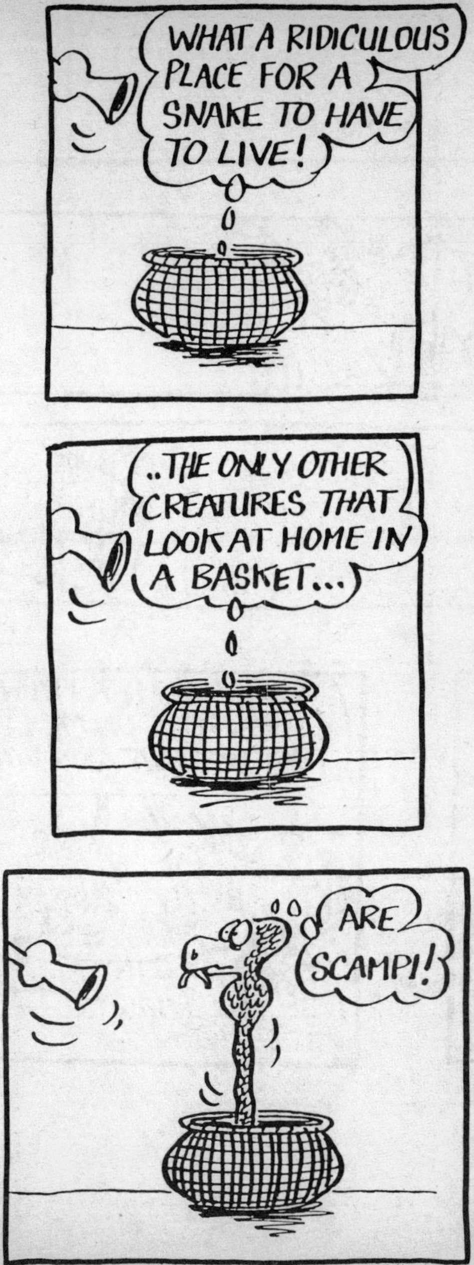
WHAT A RIDICULOUS PLACE FOR A SNAKE TO HAVE TO LIVE!
..THE ONLY OTHER CREATURES THAT LOOK AT HOME IN A BASKET...
ARE SCAMPI!

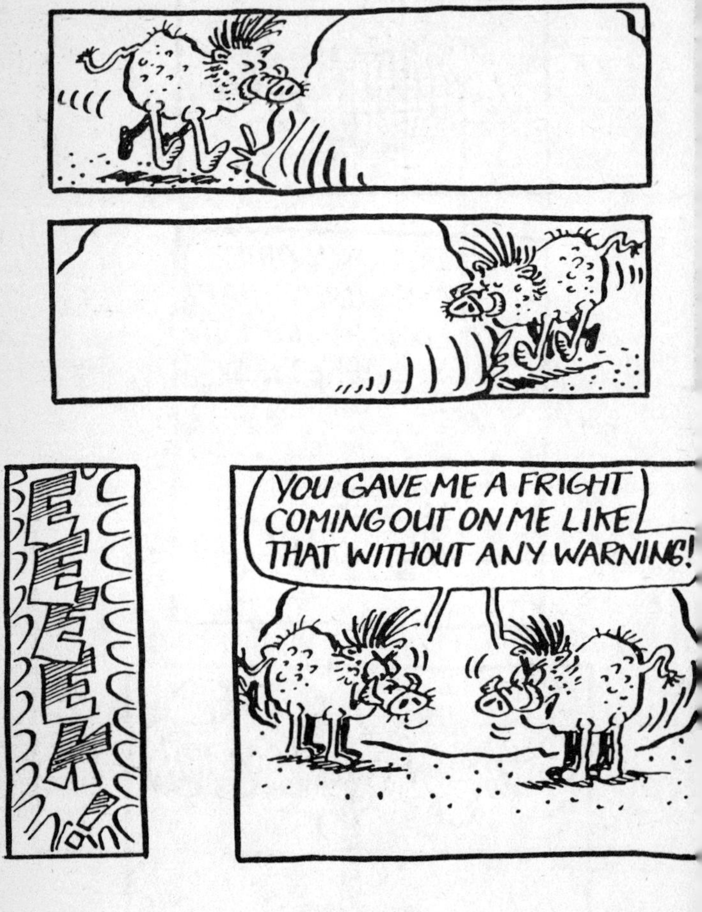
EEEEEK!
YOU GAVE ME A FRIGHT COMING OUT ON ME LIKE THAT WITHOUT ANY WARNING!

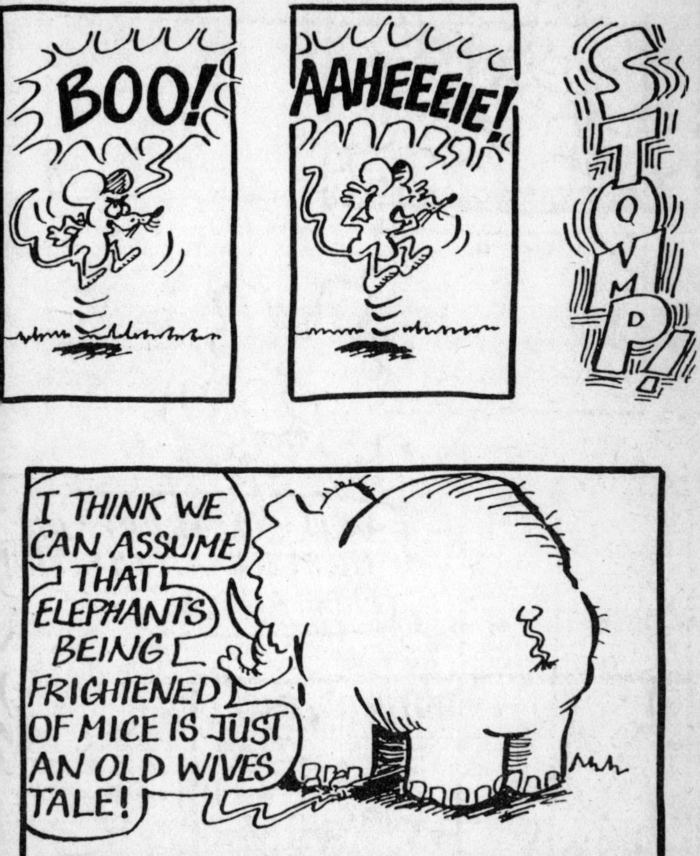
BOO!
AAHEEEEIE!
STOMP!
I THINK WE CAN ASSUME THAT ELEPHANTS BEING FRIGHTENED OF MICE IS JUST AN OLD WIVES TALE!

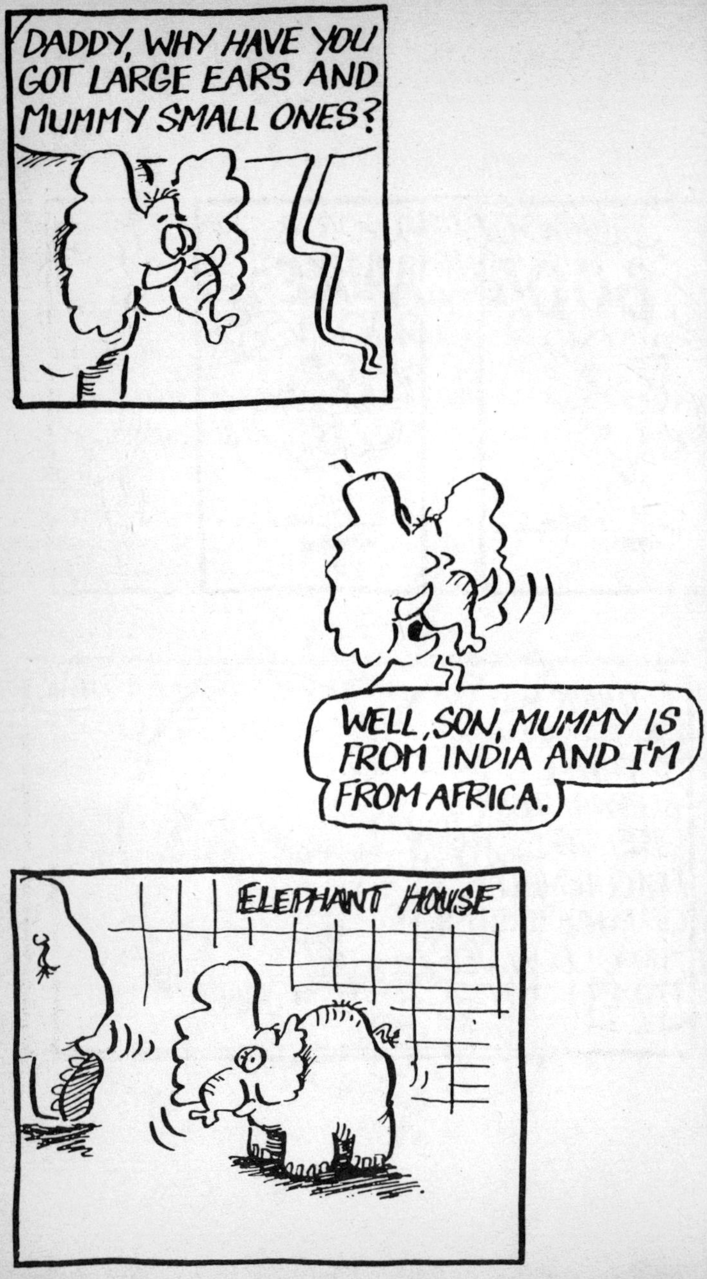
DADDY, WHY HAVE YOU GOT LARGE EARS AND MUMMY SMALL ONES?
WELL, SON, MUMMY IS FROM INDIA AND I'M FROM AFRICA.
ELEPHANT HOUSE

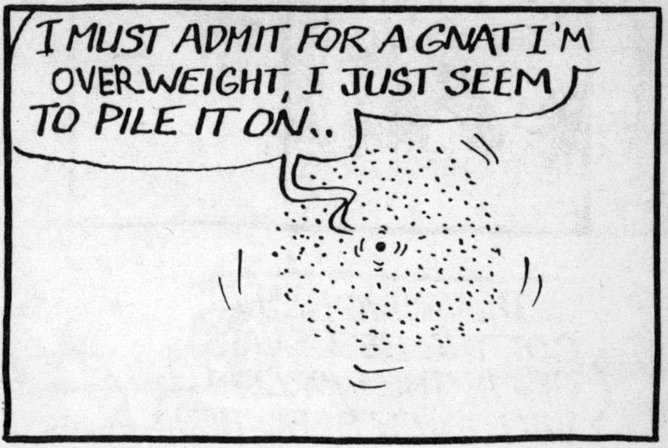
I MUST ADMIT FOR A GNAT I'M OVERWEIGHT, I JUST SEEM TO PILE IT ON..

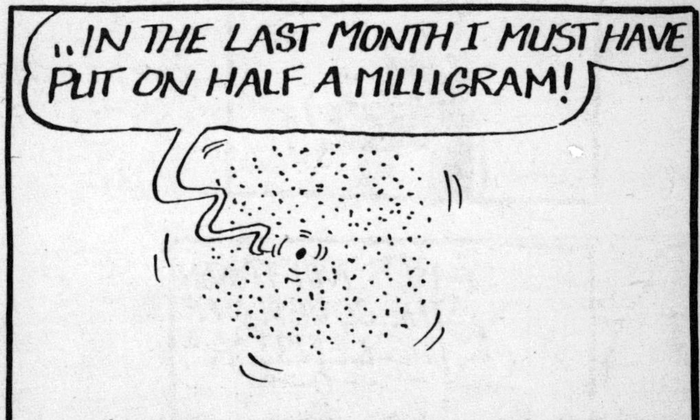
..IN THE LAST MONTH I MUST HAVE PUT ON HALF A MILLIGRAM!

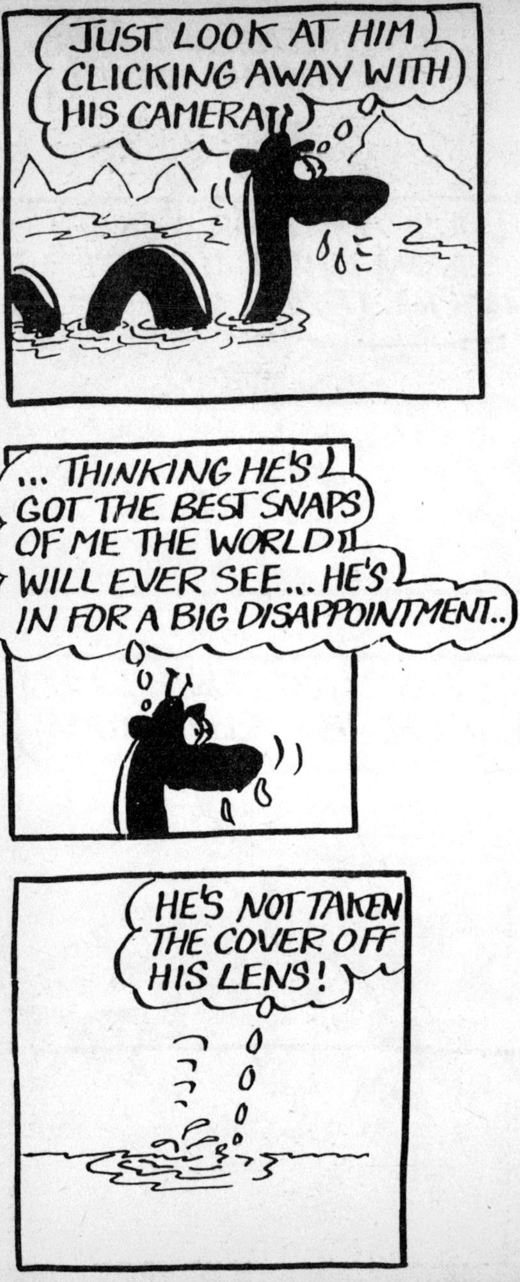
JUST LOOK AT HIM CLICKING AWAY WITH HIS CAMERA
... THINKING HE'S GOT THE BEST SNAPS OF ME THE WORLD WILL EVER SEE... HE'S IN FOR A BIG DISAPPOINTMENT..
HE'S NOT TAKEN THE COVER OFF HIS LENS!

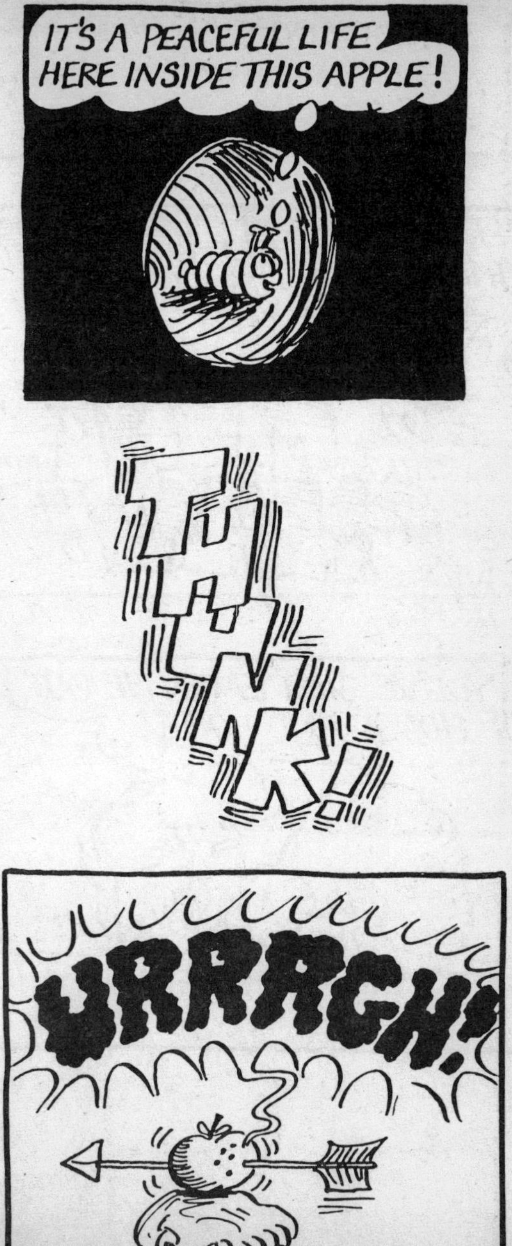
IT'S A PEACEFUL LIFE HERE INSIDE THIS APPLE!
THUNK!
URRAGH!

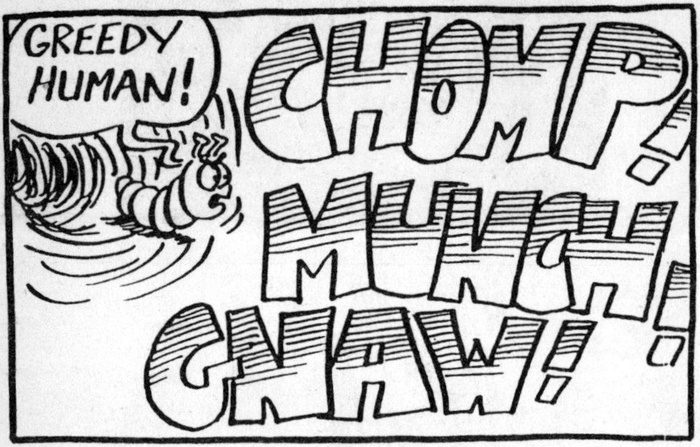
GREEDY HUMAN!
CHOMP! MUNCH! GNAW!

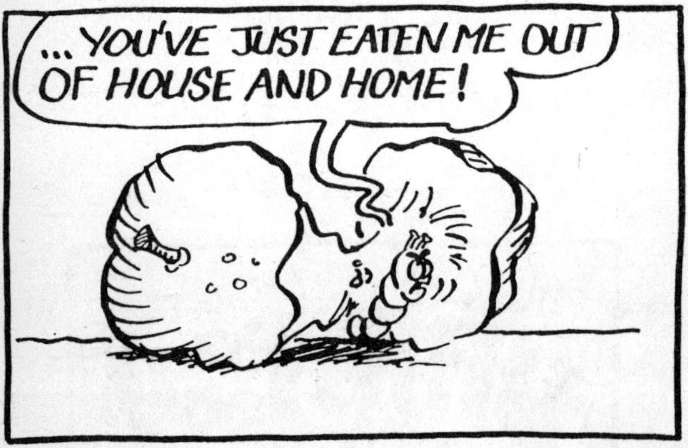
...YOU'VE JUST EATEN ME OUT OF HOUSE AND HOME!

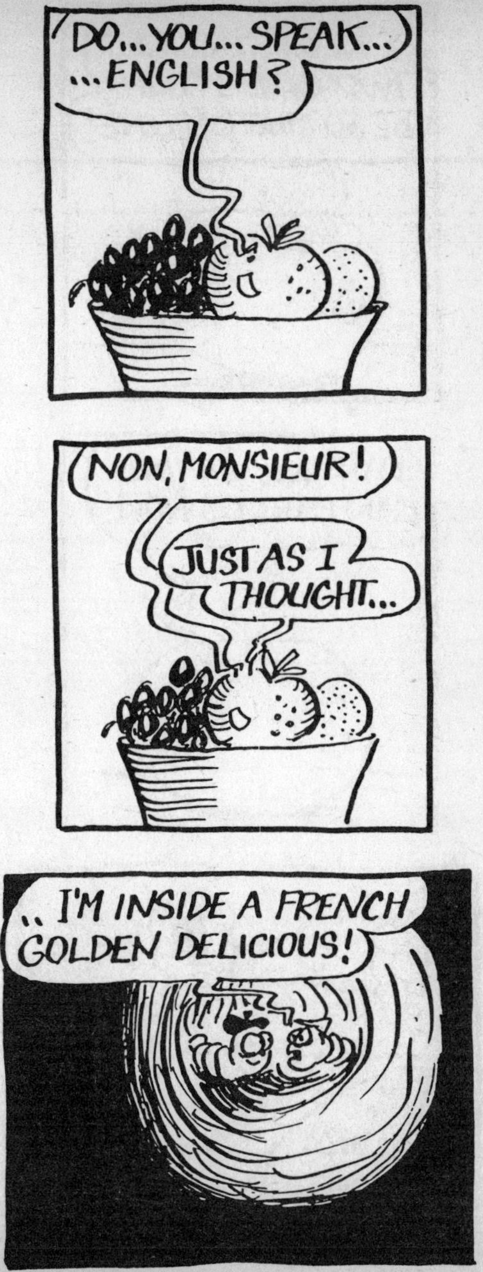
DO... YOU... SPEAK... ...ENGLISH?
NON, MONSIEUR!
JUST AS I THOUGHT...
.. I'M INSIDE A FRENCH GOLDEN DELICIOUS!

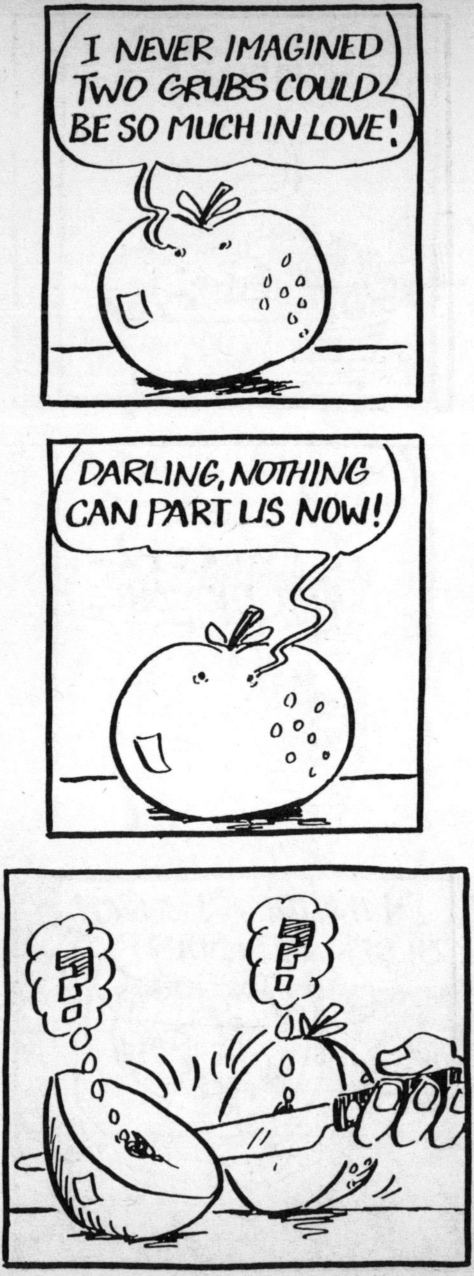
I NEVER IMAGINED TWO GRUBS COULD BE SO MUCH IN LOVE!
DARLING, NOTHING CAN PART US NOW!
?
?

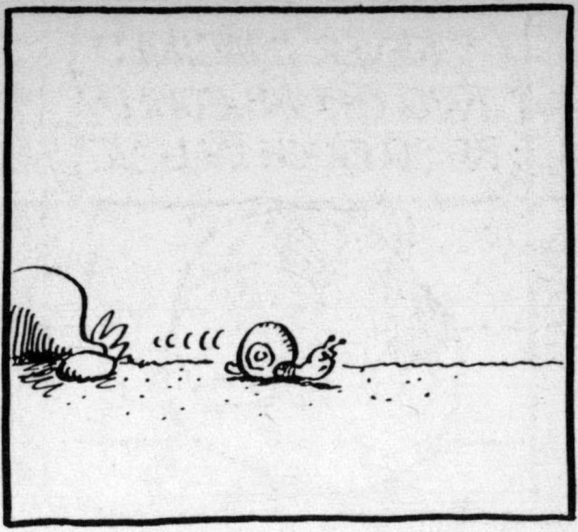

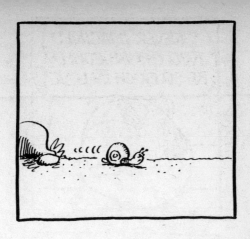

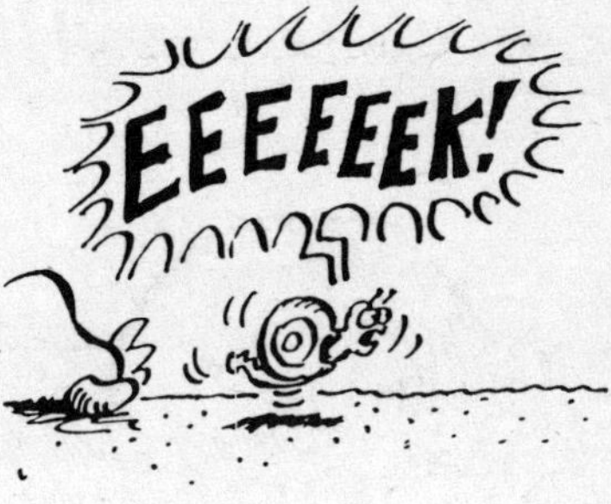
EEEEEEK!

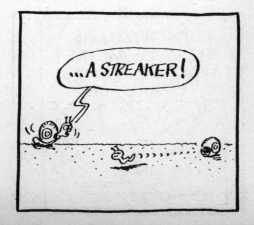

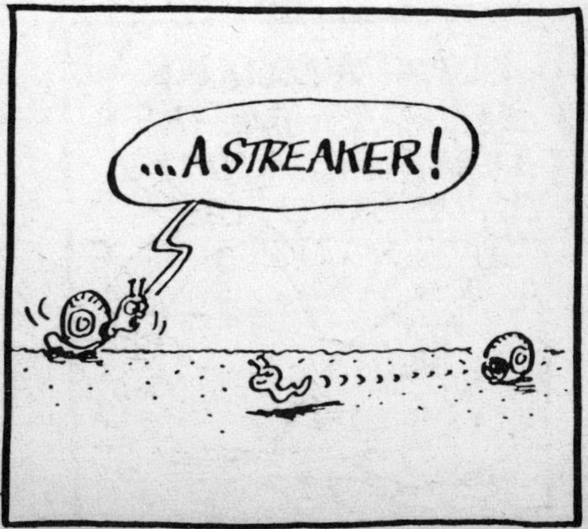
...A STREAKER!

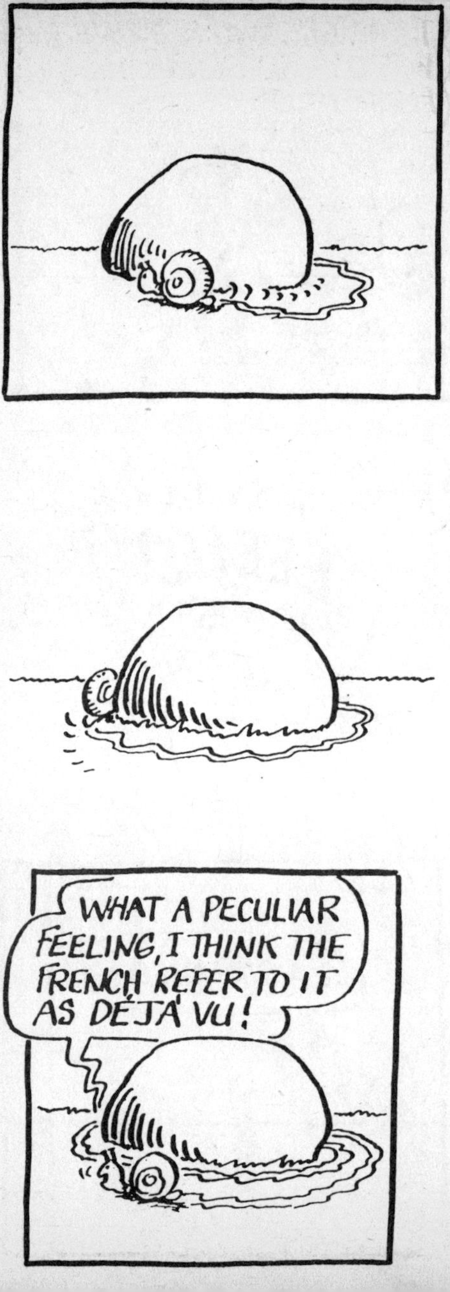
WHAT A PECULIAR FEELING, I THINK THE FRENCH REFER TO IT AS DÉJÁ VU!

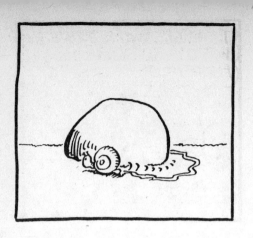

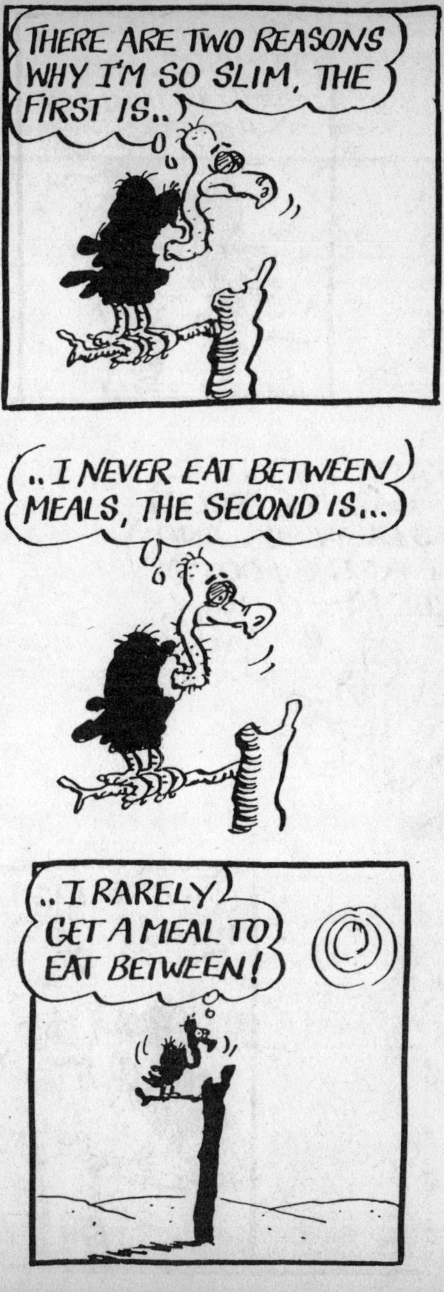
THERE ARE TWO REASONS WHY I'M SO SLIM, THE FIRST IS..
.. I NEVER EAT BETWEEN MEALS, THE SECOND IS...
.. I RARELY GET A MEAL TO EAT BETWEEN!

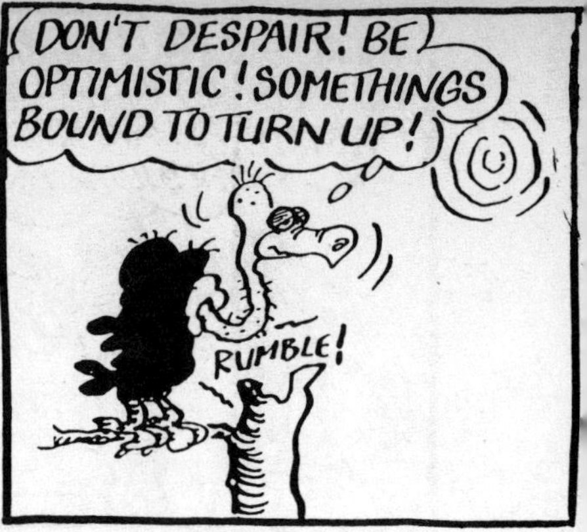
DON'T DESPAIR! BE OPTIMISTIC! SOMETHINGS BOUND TO TURN UP!
RUMBLE!

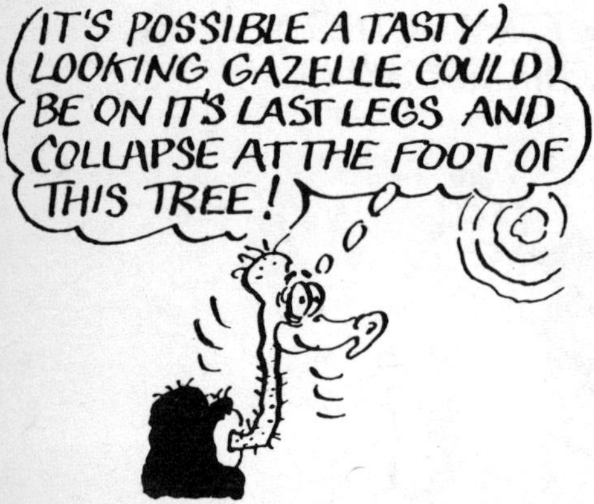
IT'S POSSIBLE A TASTY LOOKING GAZELLE COULD BE ON IT'S LAST LEGS AND COLLAPSE AT THE FOOT OF THIS TREE!

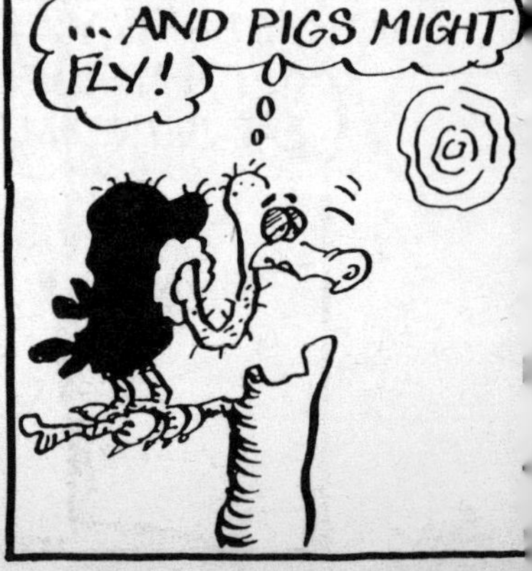
...AND PIGS MIGHT FLY!

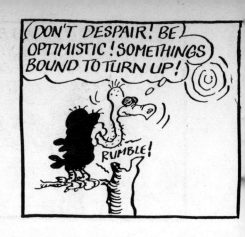

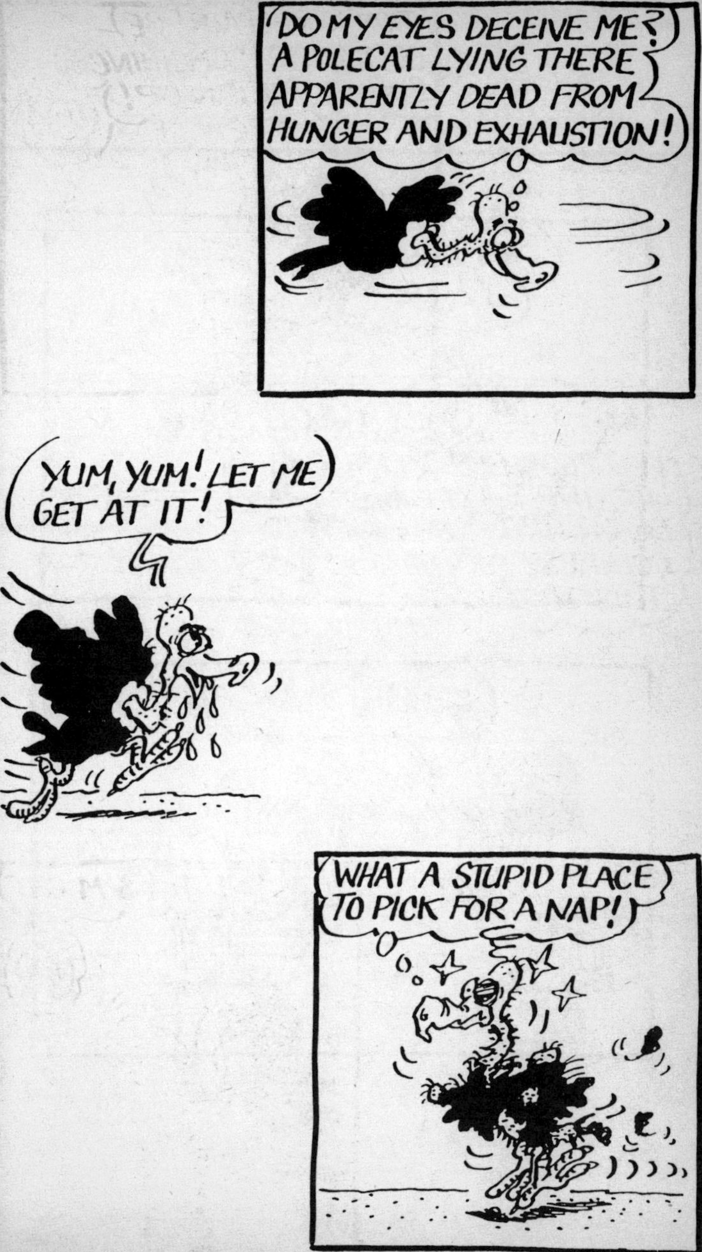
DO MY EYES DECEIVE ME? A POLECAT LYING THERE APPARENTLY DEAD FROM HUNGER AND EXHAUSTION!
YUM, YUM! LET ME GET AT IT!
WHAT A STUPID PLACE TO PICK FOR A NAP!

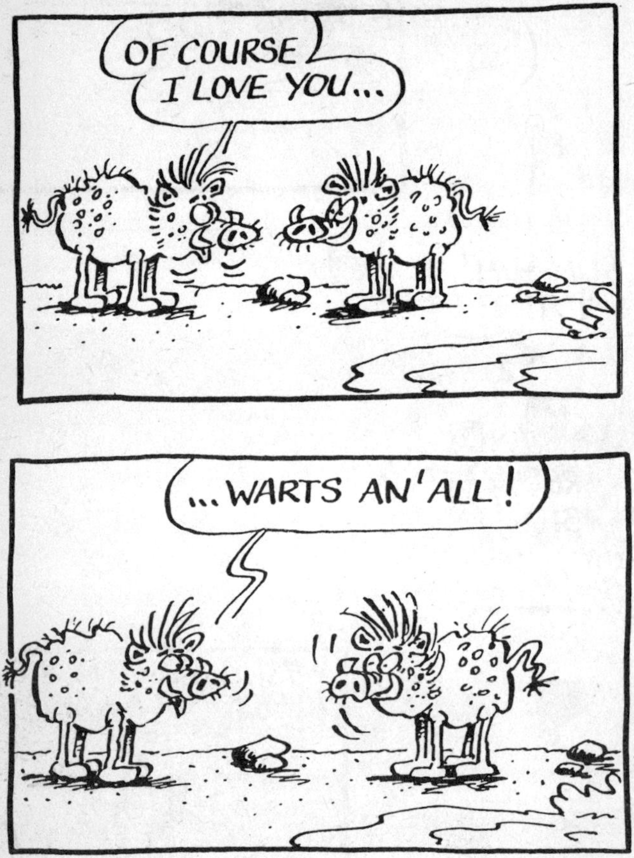
OF COURSE I LOVE YOU...
...WARTS AN'ALL!

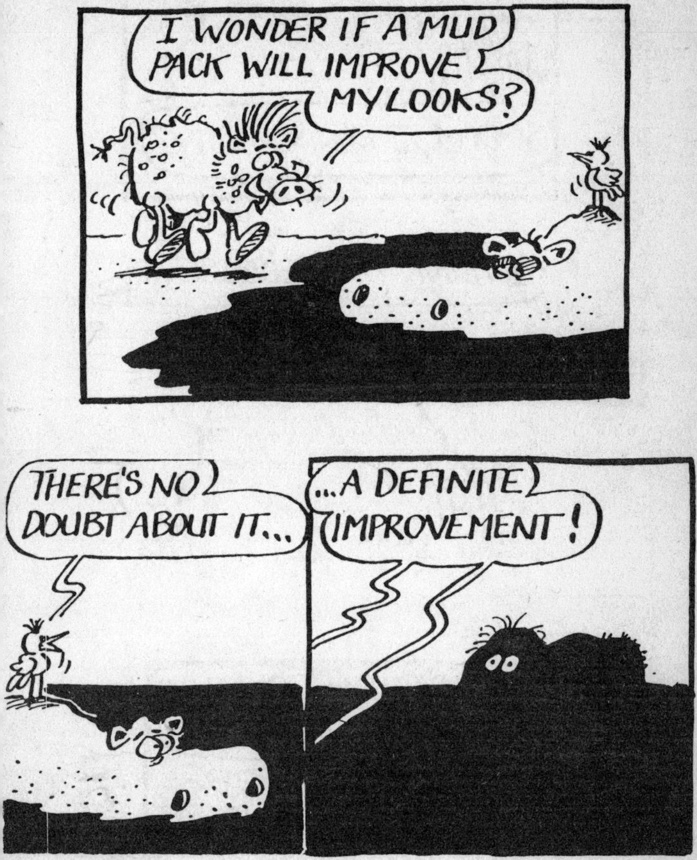
I WONDER IF A MUD PACK WILL IMPROVE MY LOOKS?
THERE'S NO DOUBT ABOUT IT...
...A DEFINITE IMPROVEMENT!

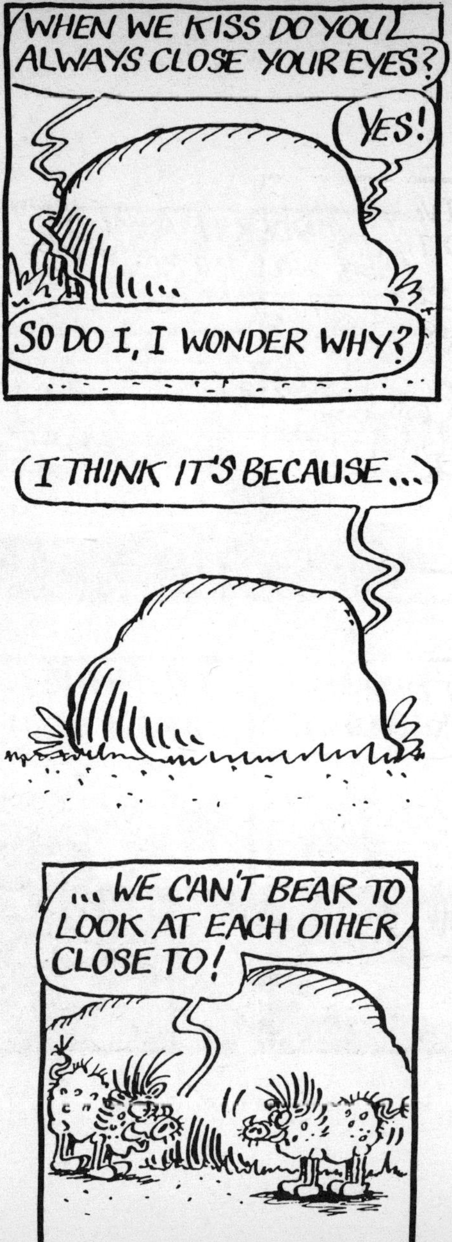
WHEN WE KISS DO YOU ALWAYS CLOSE YOUR EYES?
YES!
SO DO I, I WONDER WHY?
I THINK IT'S BECAUSE...
... WE CAN'T BEAR TO LOOK AT EACH OTHER CLOSE TO!

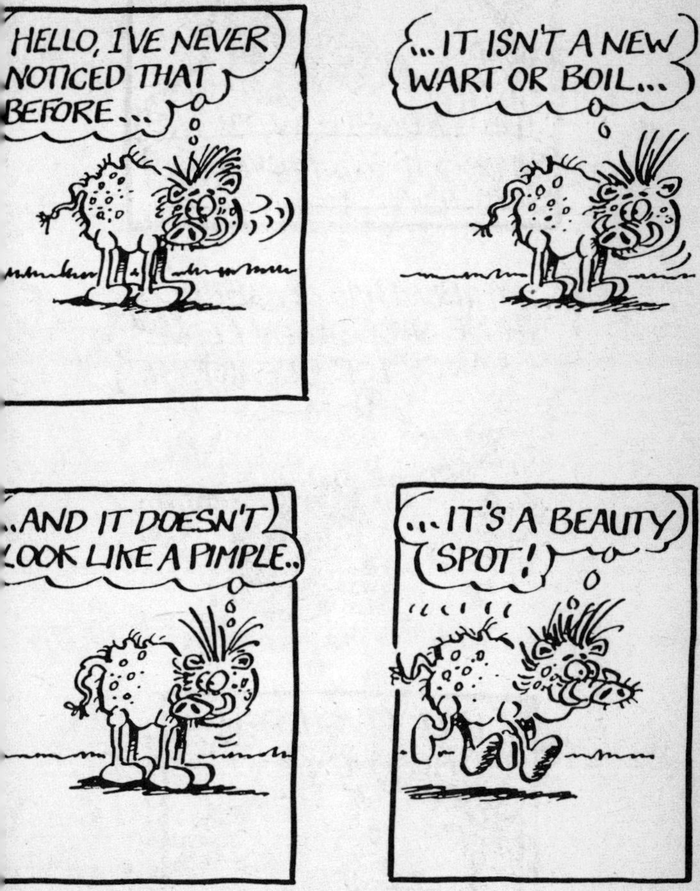
HELLO, IVE NEVER NOTICED THAT BEFORE...
...IT ISN'T A NEW WART OR BOIL...
..AND IT DOESN'T LOOK LIKE A PIMPLE..
...IT'S A BEAUTY SPOT!

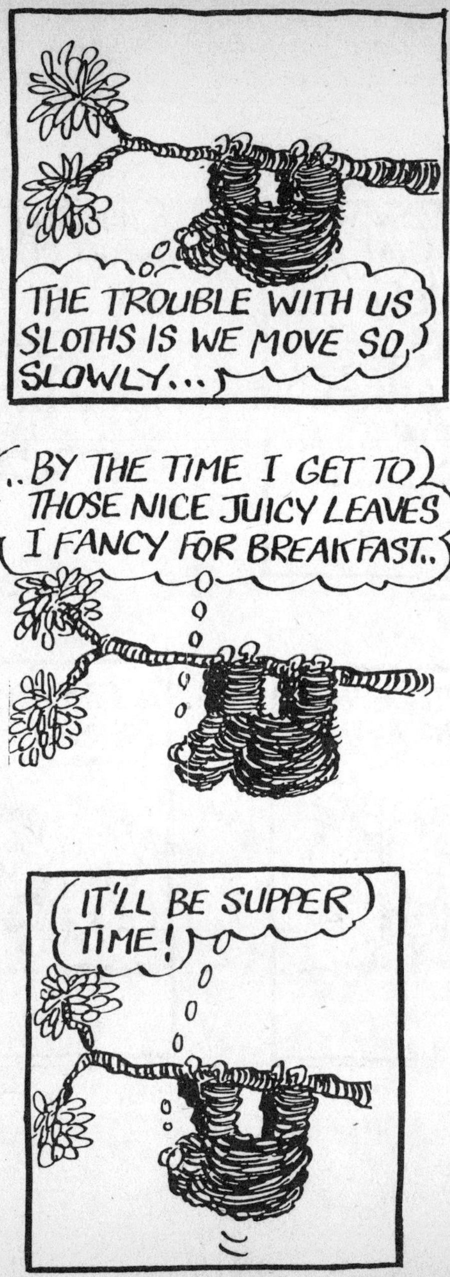
THE TROUBLE WITH US SLOTHS IS WE MOVE SO SLOWLY...
..BY THE TIME I GET TO THOSE NICE JUICY LEAVES I FANCY FOR BREAKFAST..
IT'LL BE SUPPER TIME!

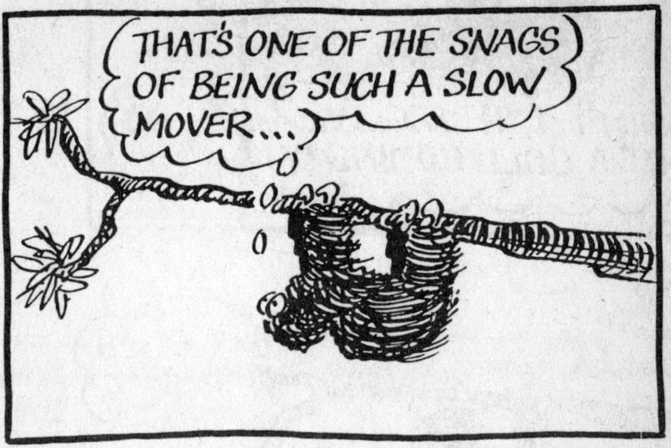
THAT'S ONE OF THE SNAGS OF BEING SUCH A SLOW MOVER...

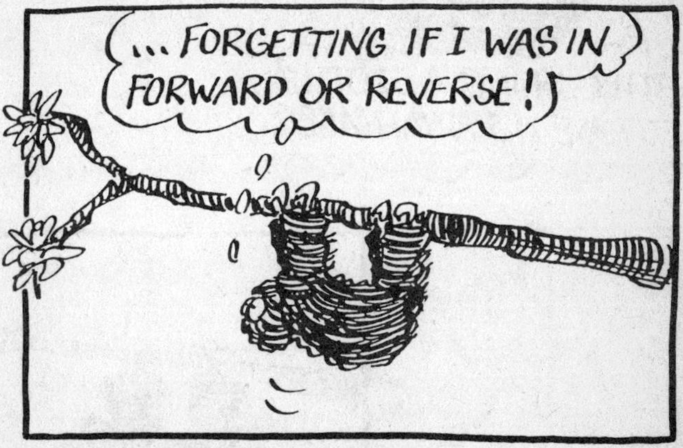
...FORGETTING IF I WAS IN FORWARD OR REVERSE!

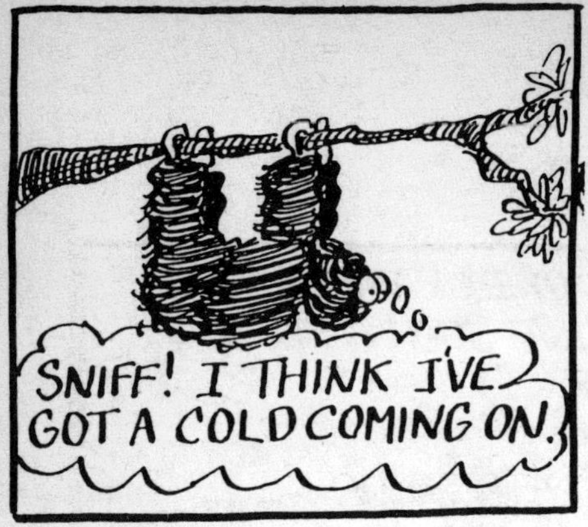
SNIFF! I THINK I'VE GOT A COLD COMING ON.

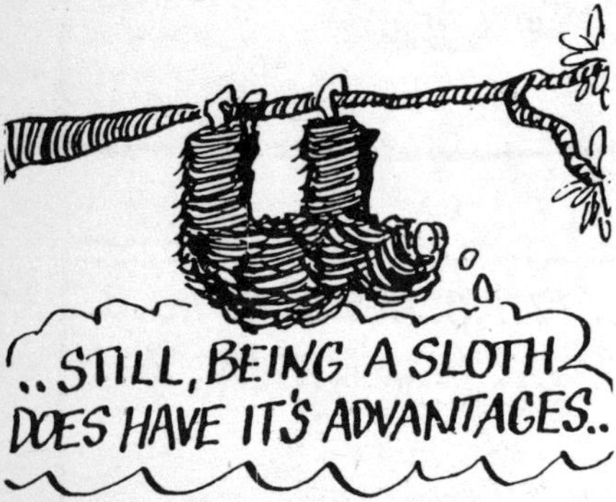
..STILL, BEING A SLOTH DOES HAVE IT'S ADVANTAGES..

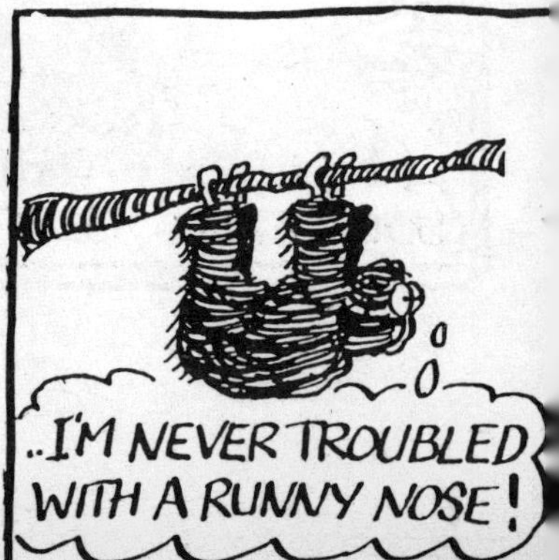
..I'M NEVER TROUBLED WITH A RUNNY NOSE!

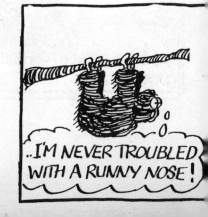

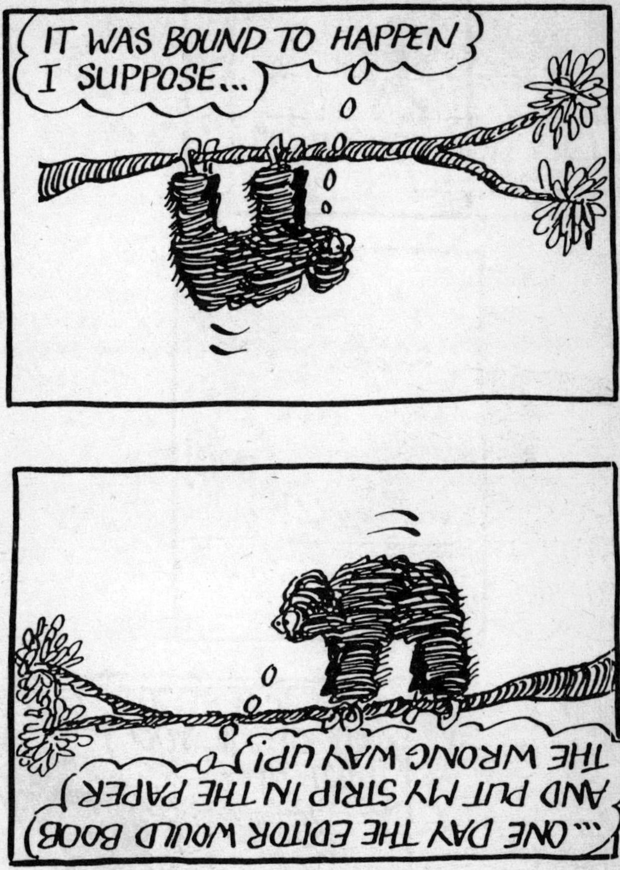
IT WAS BOUND TO HAPPEN I SUPPOSE...
...ONE DAY THE EDITOR WOULD BOOB AND PUT MY STRIP IN THE PAPER THE WRONG WAY UP!

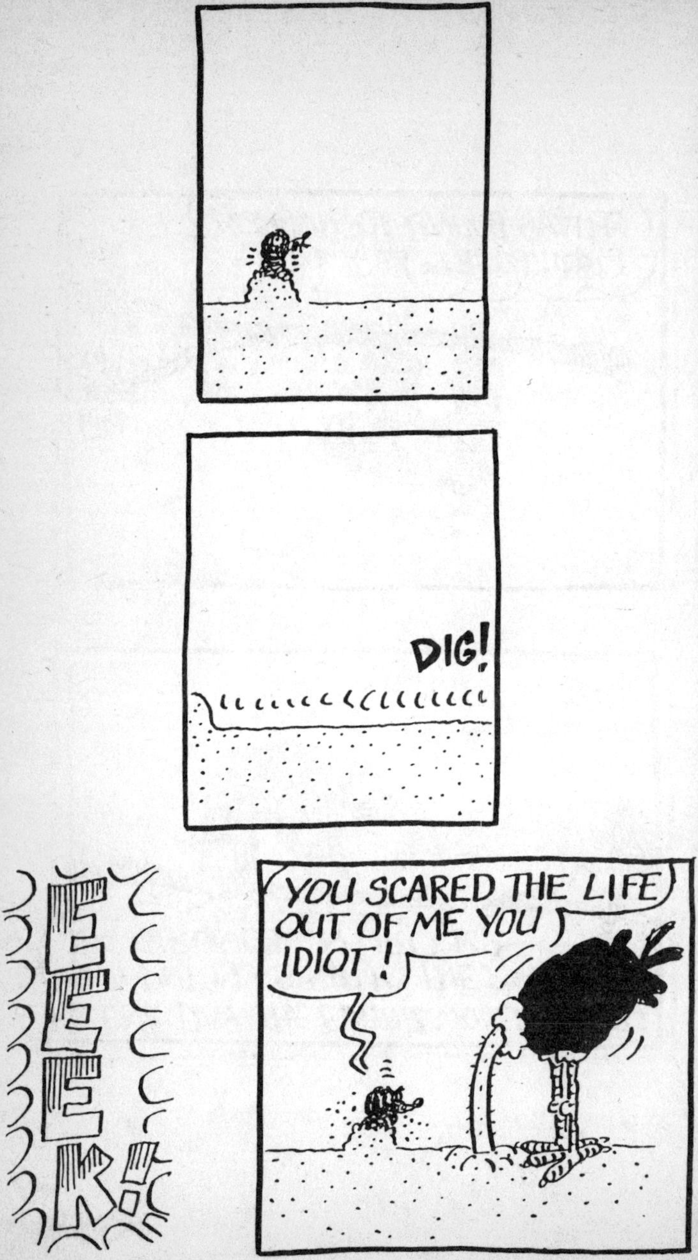
DIG!
EEEK!
YOU SCARED THE LIFE OUT OF ME YOU IDIOT!

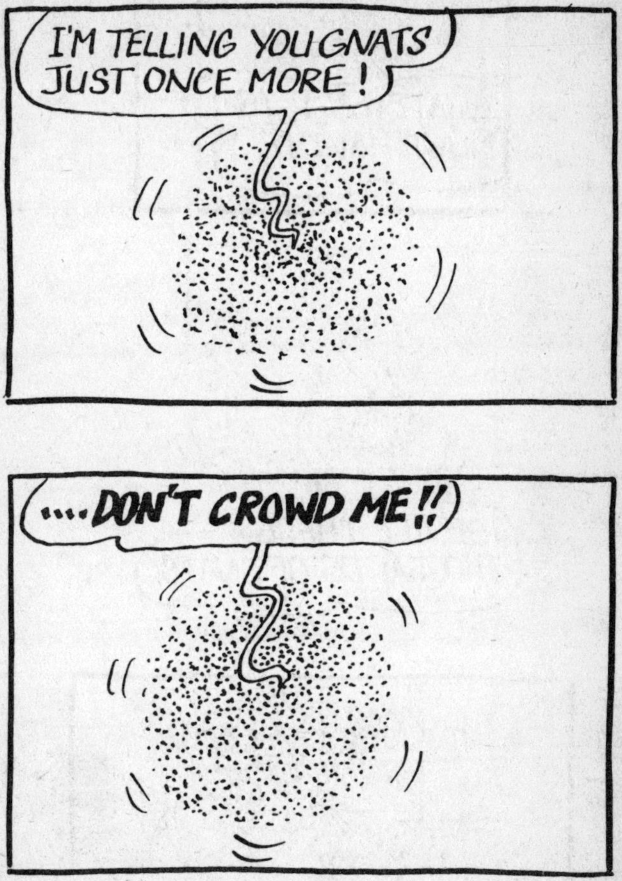
I'M TELLING YOU GNATS JUST ONCE MORE!
....DON'T CROWD ME!!

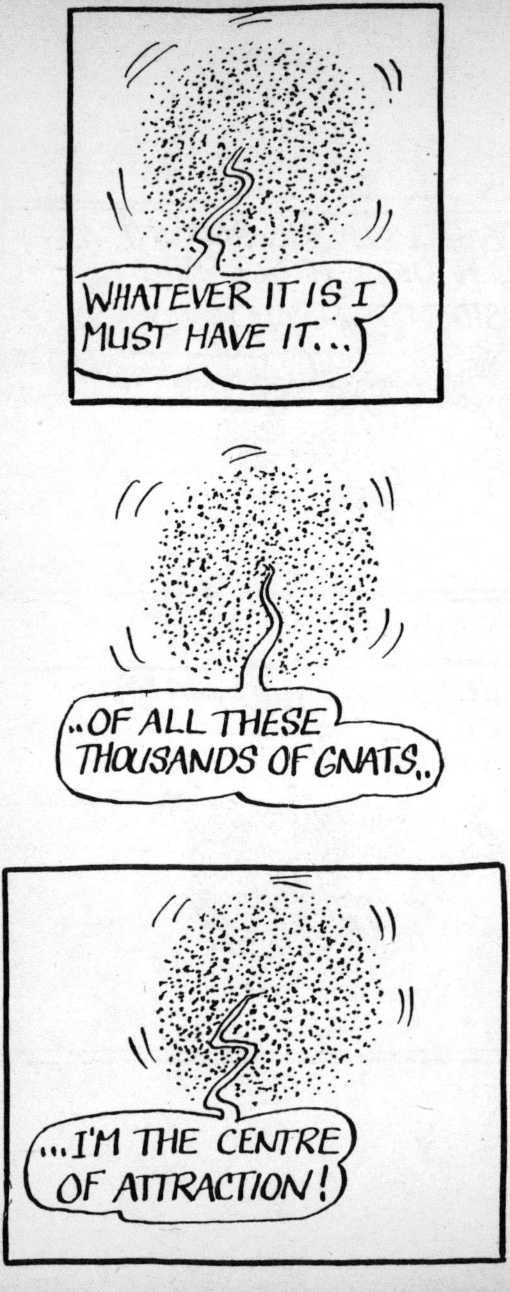
WHATEVER IT IS I MUST HAVE IT...
..OF ALL THESE THOUSANDS OF GNATS..
...I'M THE CENTRE OF ATTRACTION!

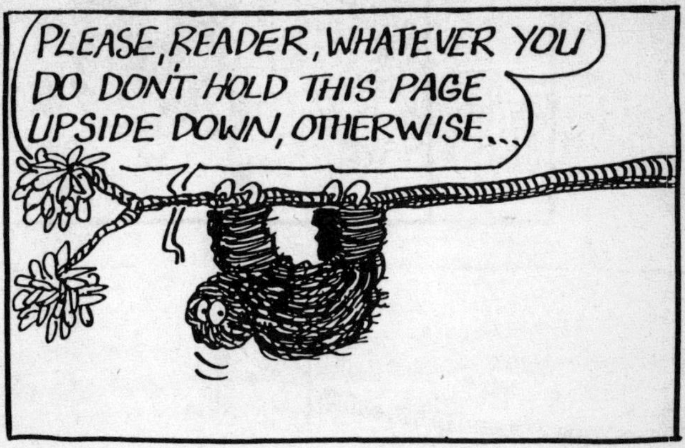
PLEASE, READER, WHATEVER YOU DO DON'T HOLD THIS PAGE UPSIDE DOWN, OTHERWISE...

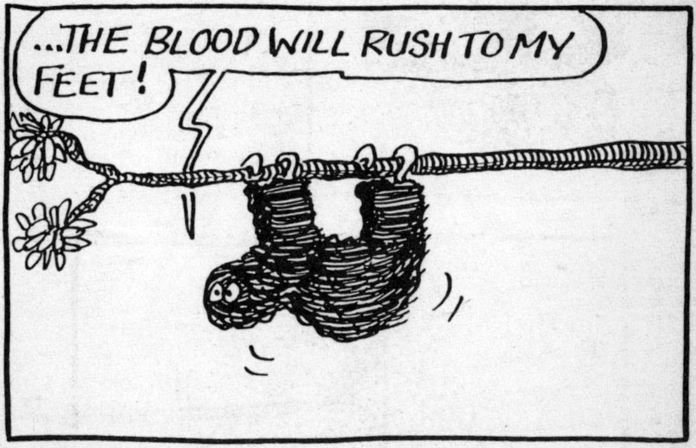
...THE BLOOD WILL RUSH TO MY FEET!

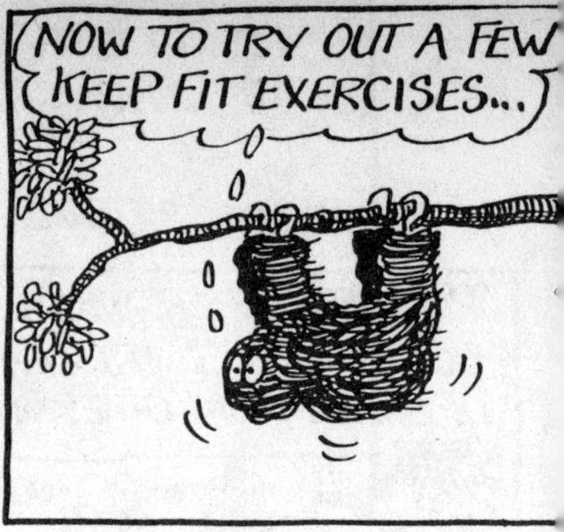
NOW TO TRY OUT A FEW KEEP FIT EXERCISES...

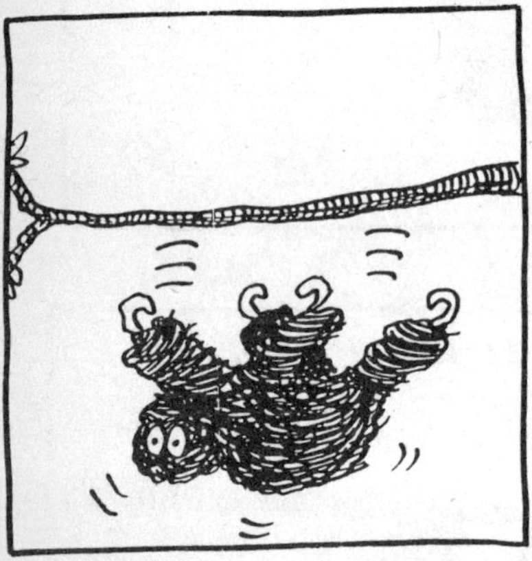

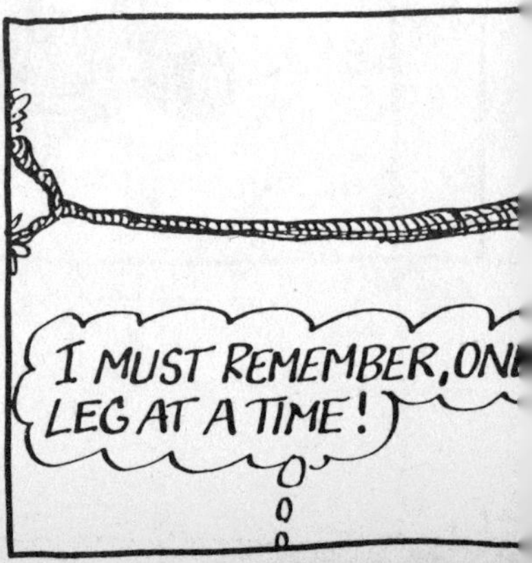
I MUST REMEMBER, ONE LEG AT A TIME!

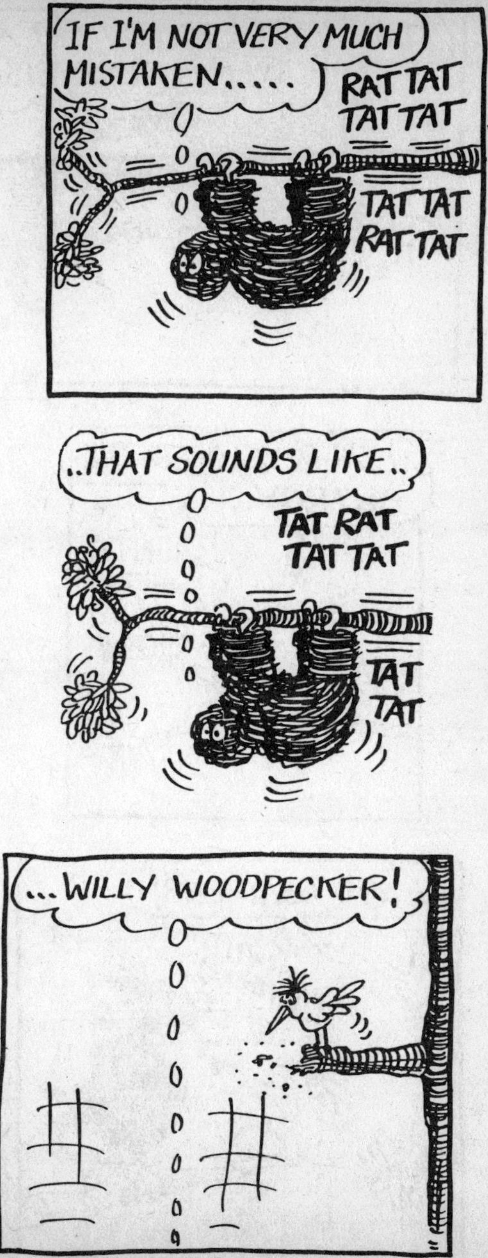
IF I'M NOT VERY MUCH MISTAKEN.....
RAT TAT TAT TAT
TAT TAT RAT TAT
..THAT SOUNDS LIKE..
TAT RAT TAT TAT
TAT TAT
...WILLY WOODPECKER!

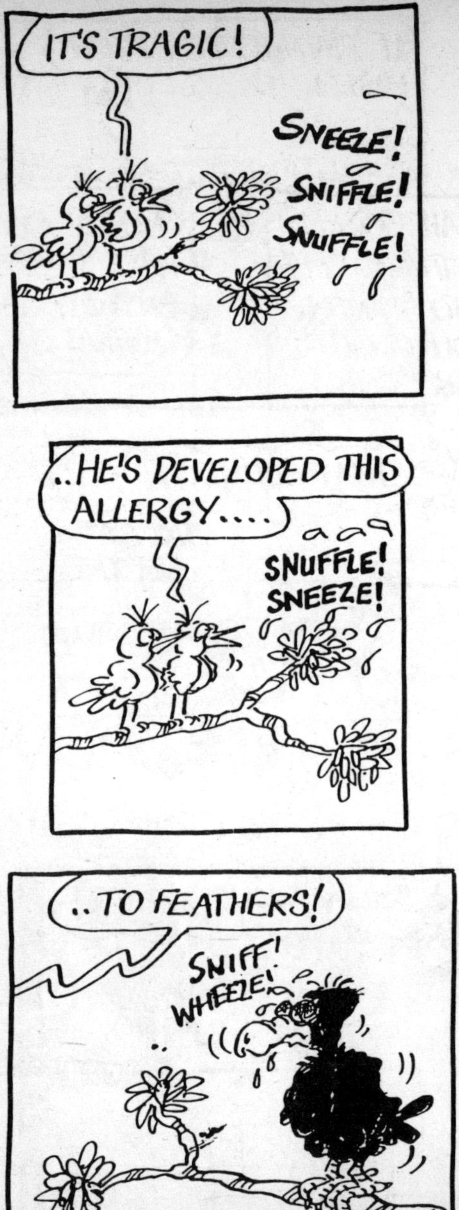
IT'S TRAGIC!
SNEEZE!
SNIFFLE!
SNUFFLE!
..HE'S DEVELOPED THIS ALLERGY....
SNUFFLE!
SNEEZE!
..TO FEATHERS!
SNIFF!
WHEEZE!

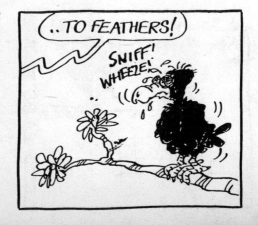

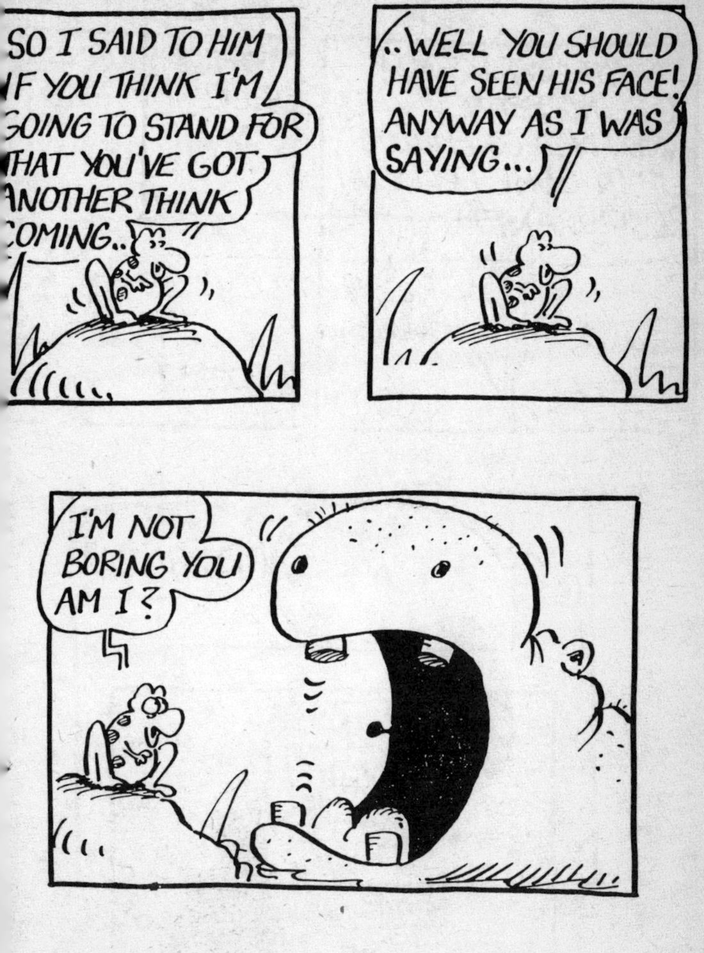
SO I SAID TO HIM IF YOU THINK I'M GOING TO STAND FOR THAT YOU'VE GOT ANOTHER THINK COMING..
..WELL YOU SHOULD HAVE SEEN HIS FACE! ANYWAY AS I WAS SAYING...
I'M NOT BORING YOU AM I?

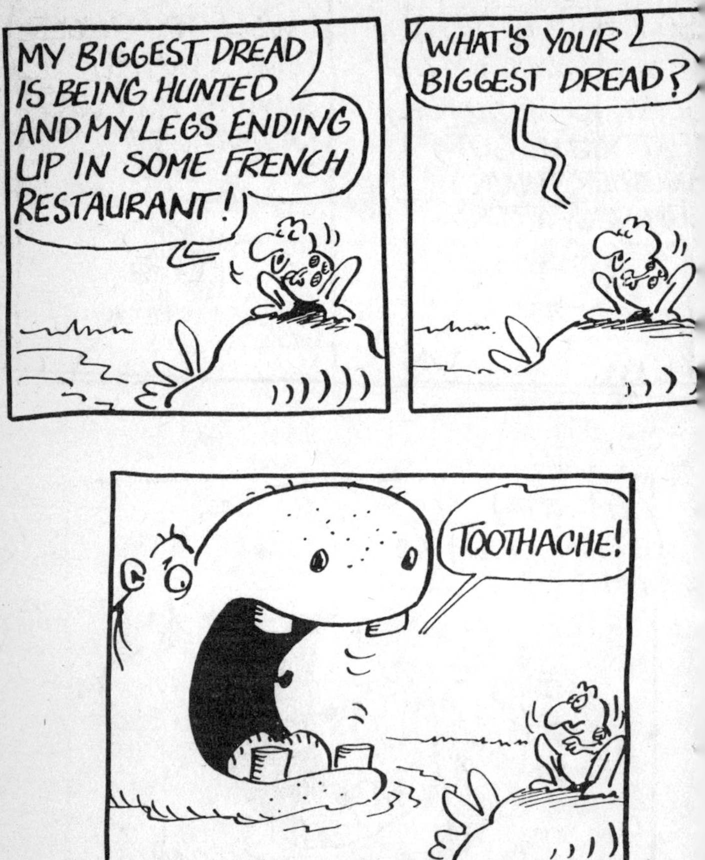
MY BIGGEST DREAD IS BEING HUNTED AND MY LEGS ENDING UP IN SOME FRENCH RESTAURANT!
WHAT'S YOUR BIGGEST DREAD?
TOOTHACHE!

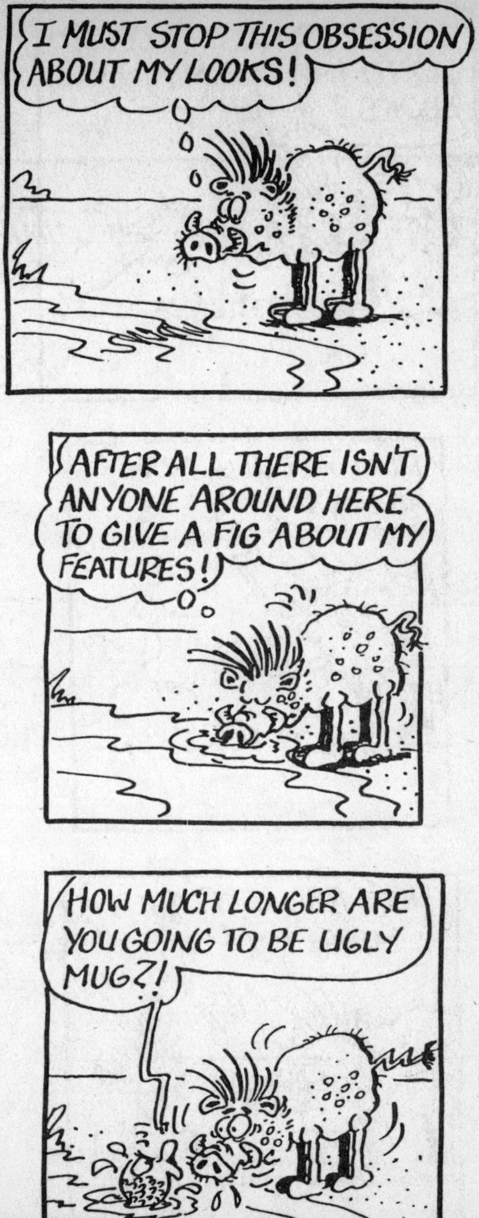
I MUST STOP THIS OBSESSION ABOUT MY LOOKS!
AFTER ALL THERE ISN'T ANYONE AROUND HERE TO GIVE A FIG ABOUT MY FEATURES!
HOW MUCH LONGER ARE YOU GOING TO BE UGLY MUG?!

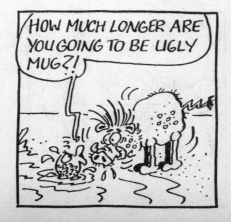

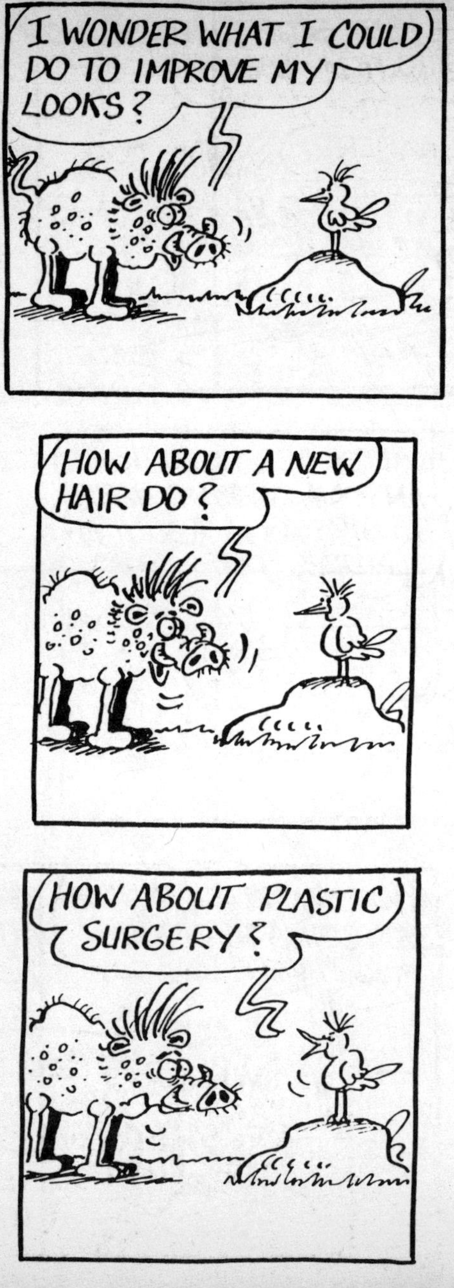
I WONDER WHAT I COULD DO TO IMPROVE MY LOOKS?
HOW ABOUT A NEW HAIR DO?
HOW ABOUT PLASTIC SURGERY?

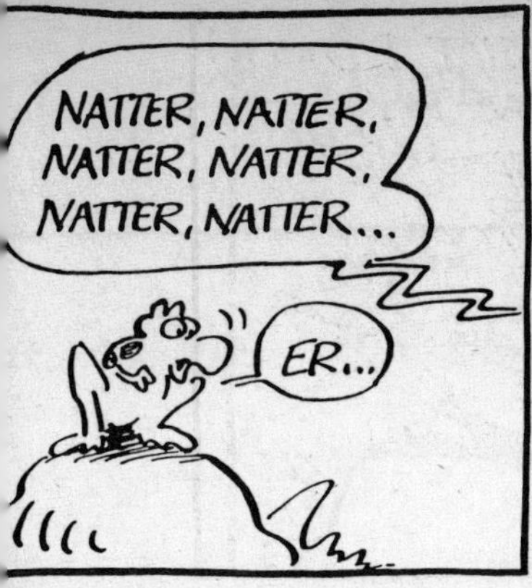
NATTER, NATTER, NATTER, NATTER, NATTER, NATTER...
ER...

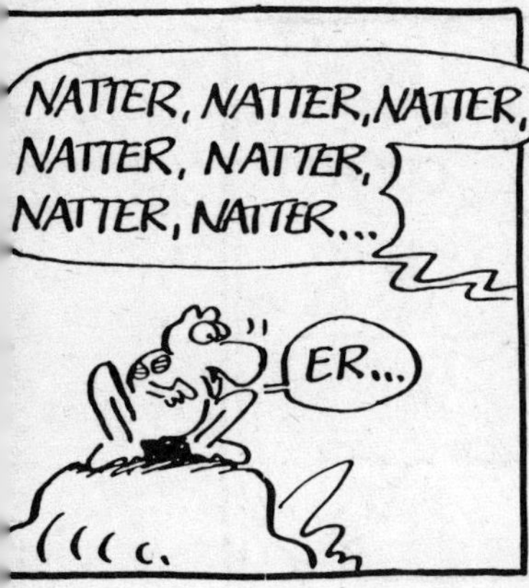
NATTER, NATTER, NATTER, NATTER, NATTER, NATTER, NATTER...
ER...

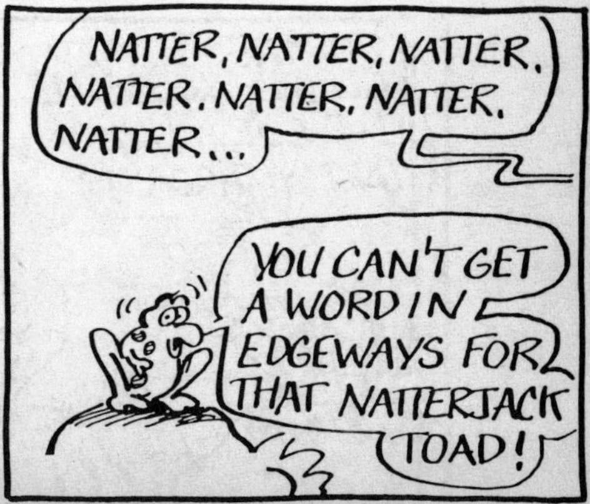
NATTER, NATTER, NATTER, NATTER. NATTER, NATTER. NATTER...
YOU CAN'T GET A WORD IN EDGEWAYS FOR THAT NATTERJACK TOAD!

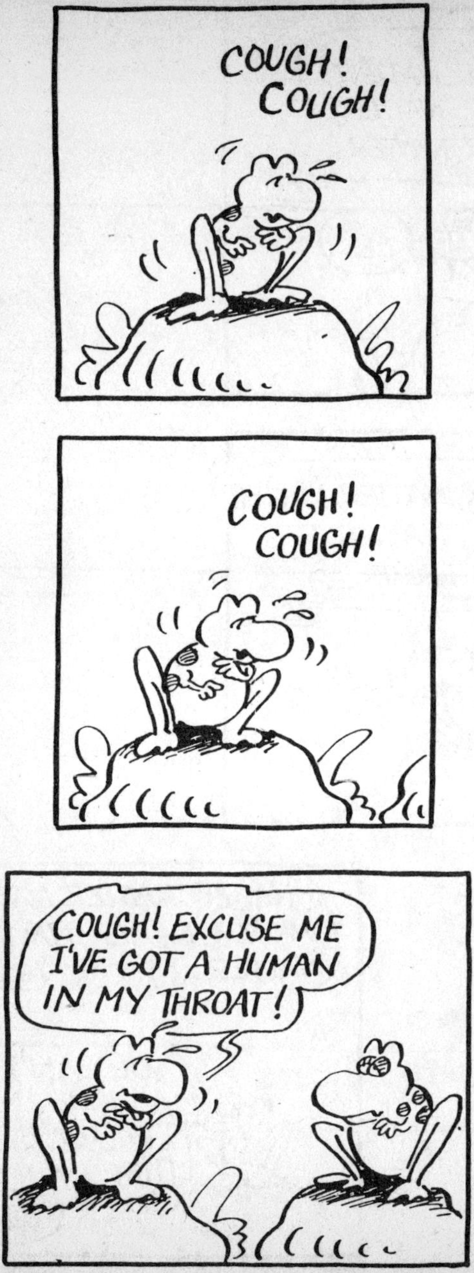
COUGH! COUGH!
COUGH! COUGH!
COUGH! EXCUSE ME I'VE GOT A HUMAN IN MY THROAT!

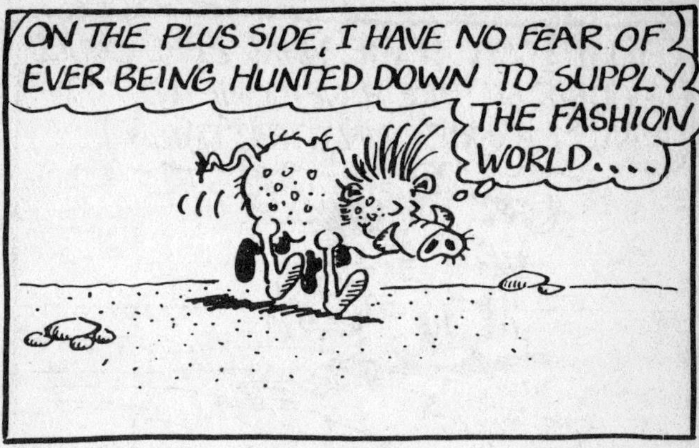
ON THE PLUS SIDE, I HAVE NO FEAR OF EVER BEING HUNTED DOWN TO SUPPLY THE FASHION WORLD....

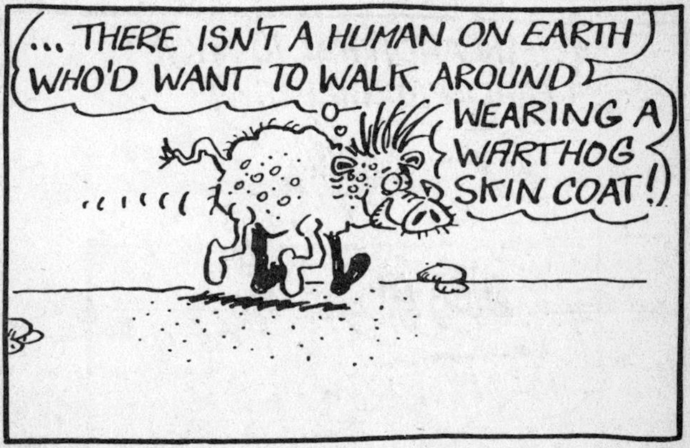
...THERE ISN'T A HUMAN ON EARTH WHO'D WANT TO WALK AROUND WEARING A WARTHOG SKIN COAT!

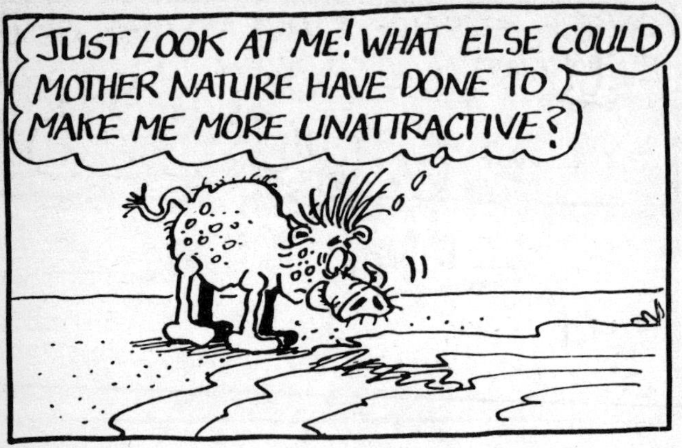
JUST LOOK AT ME! WHAT ELSE COULD MOTHER NATURE HAVE DONE TO MAKE ME MORE UNATTRACTIVE?

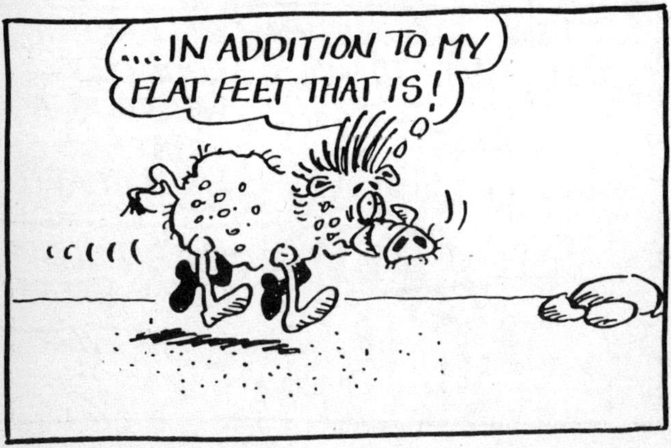
....IN ADDITION TO MY FLAT FEET THAT IS!

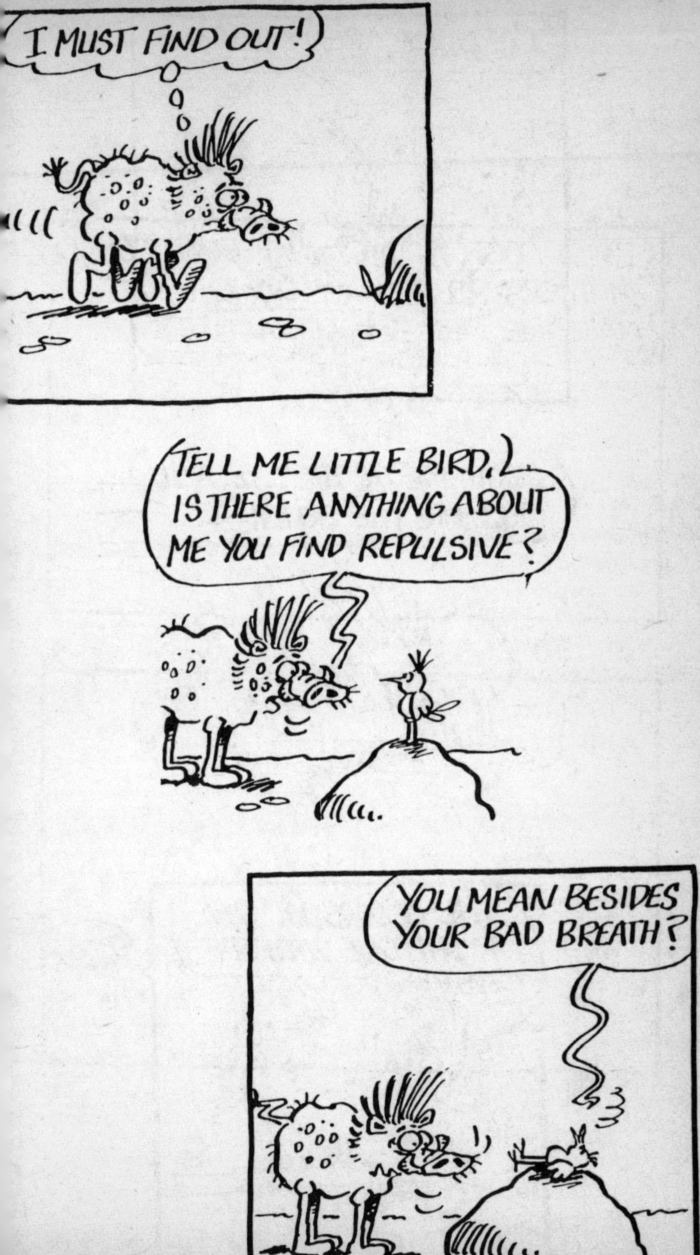
I MUST FIND OUT!
TELL ME LITTLE BIRD, IS THERE ANYTHING ABOUT ME YOU FIND REPULSIVE?
YOU MEAN BESIDES YOUR BAD BREATH?

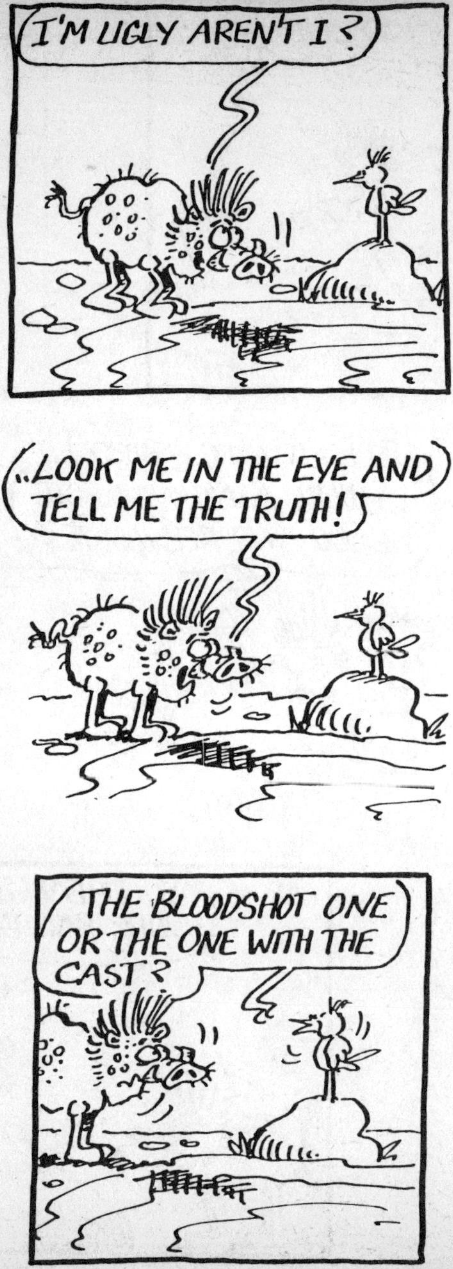
I'M UGLY AREN'T I?
..LOOK ME IN THE EYE AND TELL ME THE TRUTH!
THE BLOODSHOT ONE OR THE ONE WITH THE CAST?

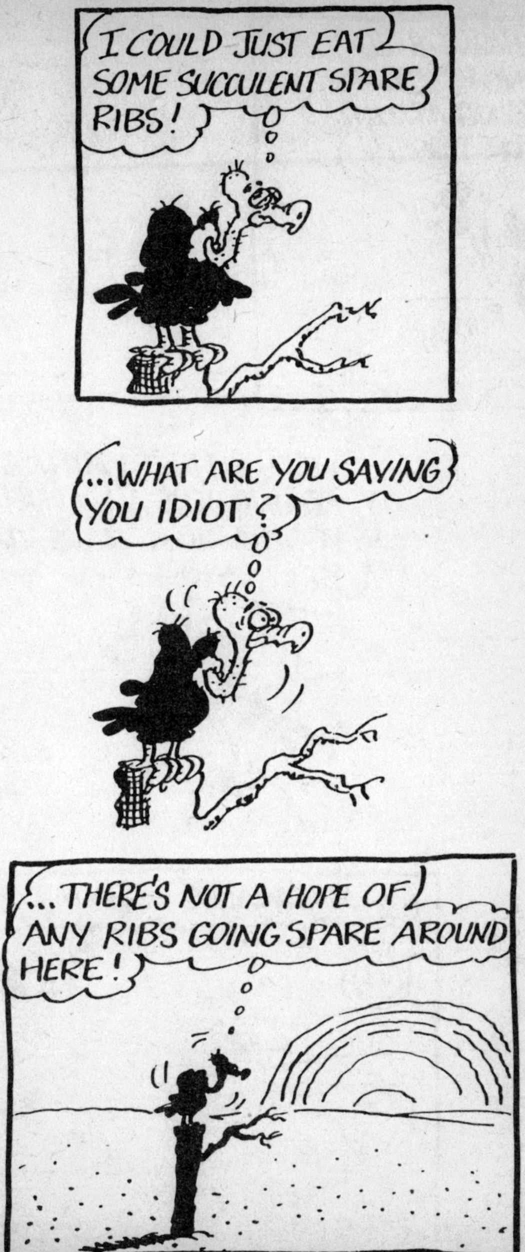
I COULD JUST EAT SOME SUCCULENT SPARE RIBS!
...WHAT ARE YOU SAYING YOU IDIOT?
...THERE'S NOT A HOPE OF ANY RIBS GOING SPARE AROUND HERE!

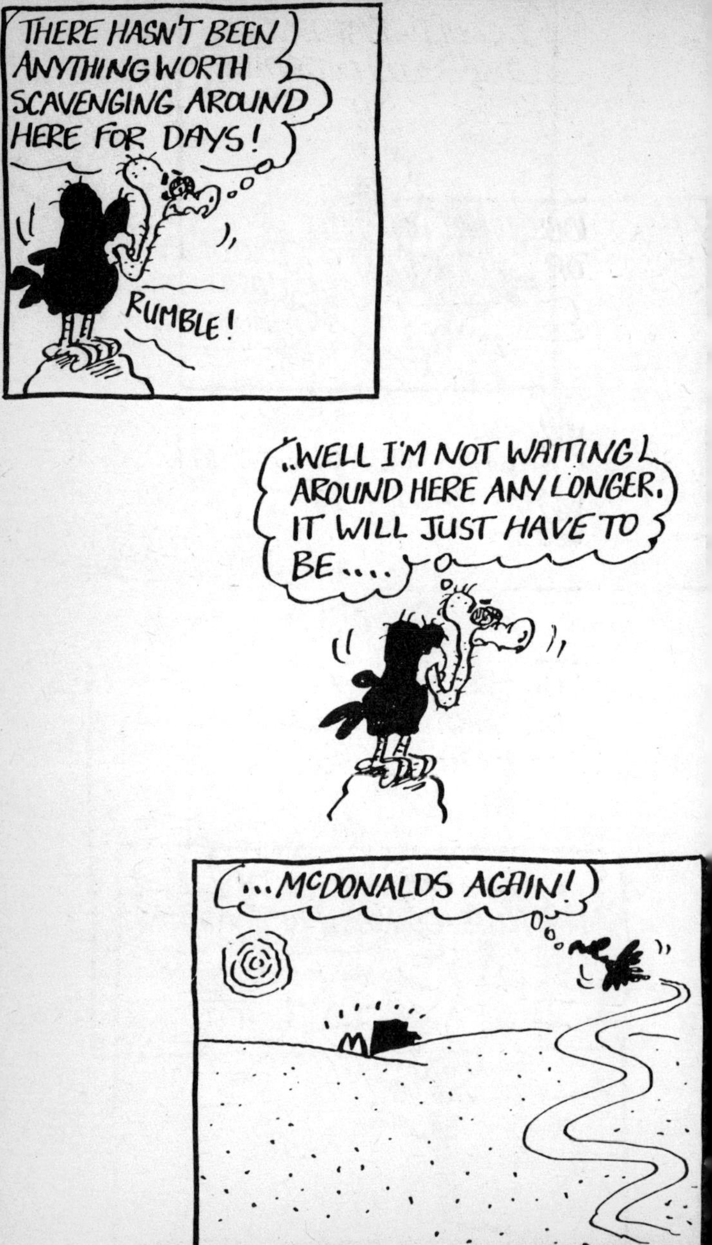
THERE HASN'T BEEN ANYTHING WORTH SCAVENGING AROUND HERE FOR DAYS!
RUMBLE!
..WELL I'M NOT WAITING AROUND HERE ANY LONGER. IT WILL JUST HAVE TO BE....
...McDONALDS AGAIN!
M

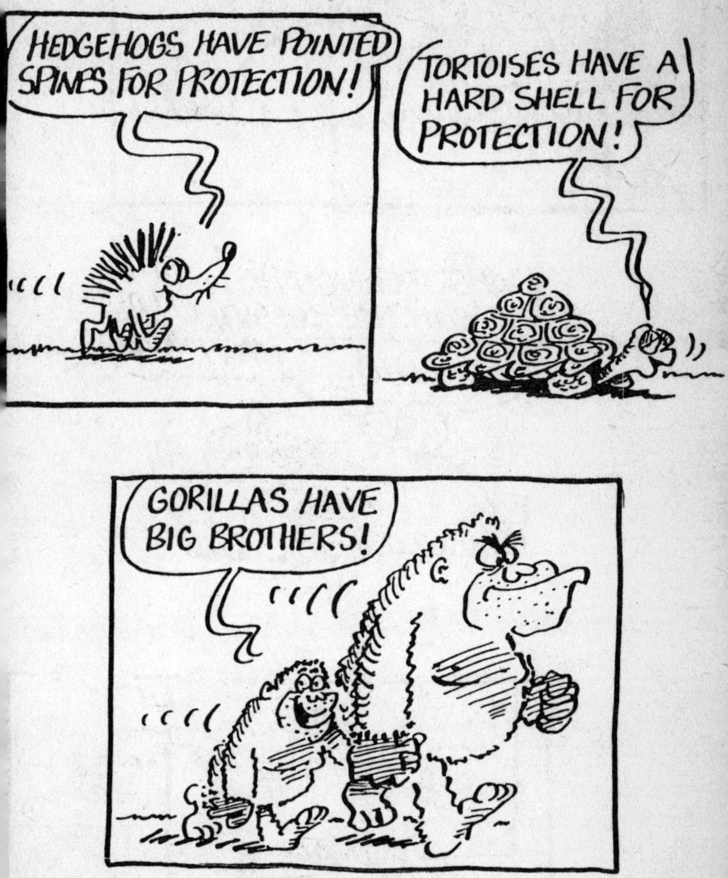
HEDGEHOGS HAVE POINTED SPINES FOR PROTECTION!
TORTOISES HAVE A HARD SHELL FOR PROTECTION!
GORILLAS HAVE BIG BROTHERS!

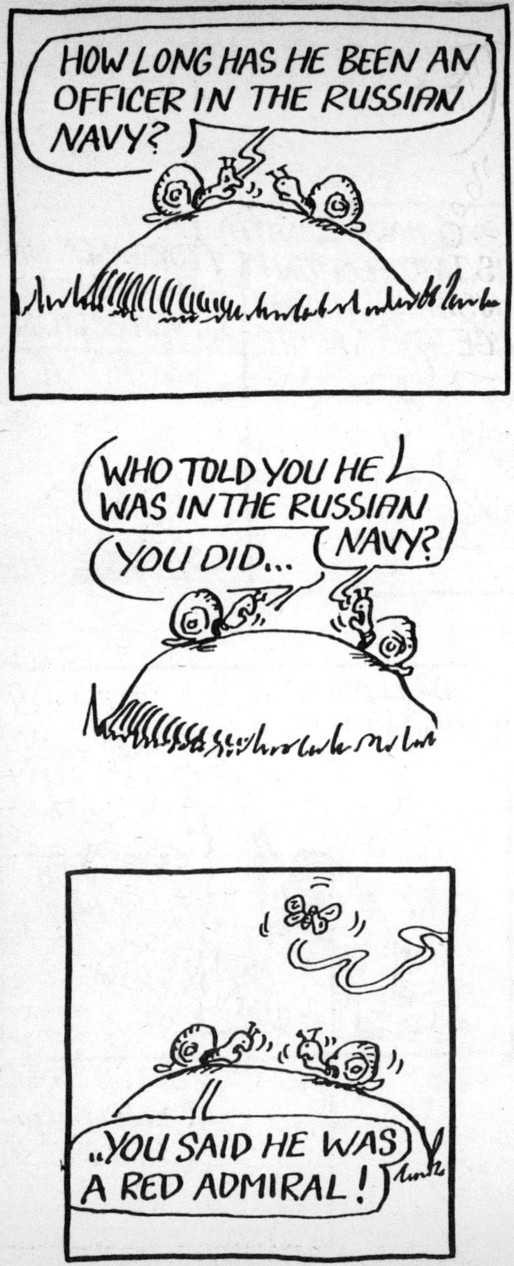
HOW LONG HAS HE BEEN AN OFFICER IN THE RUSSIAN NAVY?
WHO TOLD YOU HE WAS IN THE RUSSIAN NAVY?
YOU DID...
..YOU SAID HE WAS A RED ADMIRAL!

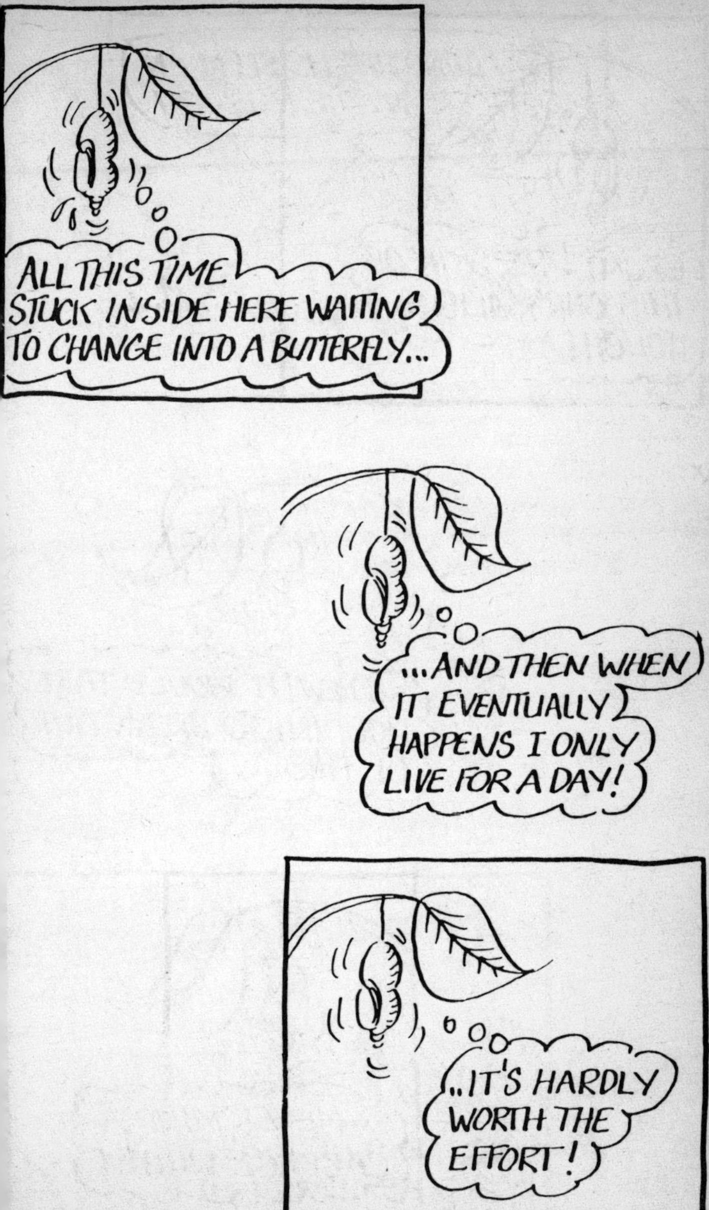
ALL THIS TIME STUCK INSIDE HERE WAITING TO CHANGE INTO A BUTTERFLY...
...AND THEN WHEN IT EVENTUALLY HAPPENS I ONLY LIVE FOR A DAY!
..IT'S HARDLY WORTH THE EFFORT!

GRUNT! THE SKIN OF THIS CHRYSALIS IS TOUGH!
...PHEW! IT WOULD TAKE HOUDINI TO BREAK OUT OF THIS...
...NEVER MIND A CABBAGE WHITE!

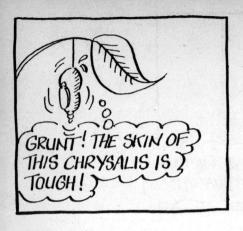

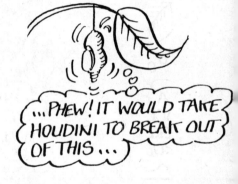

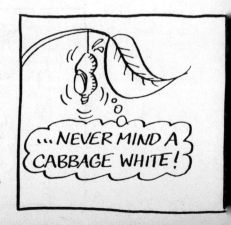

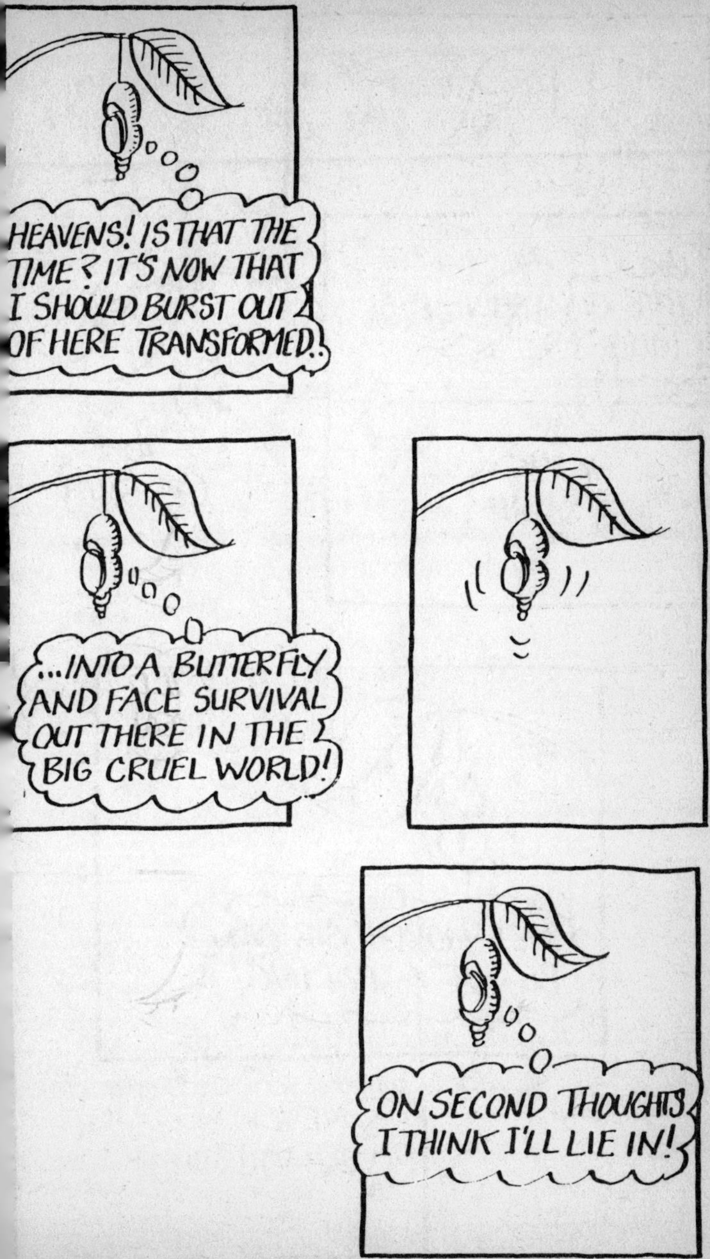
HEAVENS! IS THAT THE TIME? IT'S NOW THAT I SHOULD BURST OUT OF HERE TRANSFORMED...
...INTO A BUTTERFLY AND FACE SURVIVAL OUT THERE IN THE BIG CRUEL WORLD!
ON SECOND THOUGHTS I THINK I'LL LIE IN!

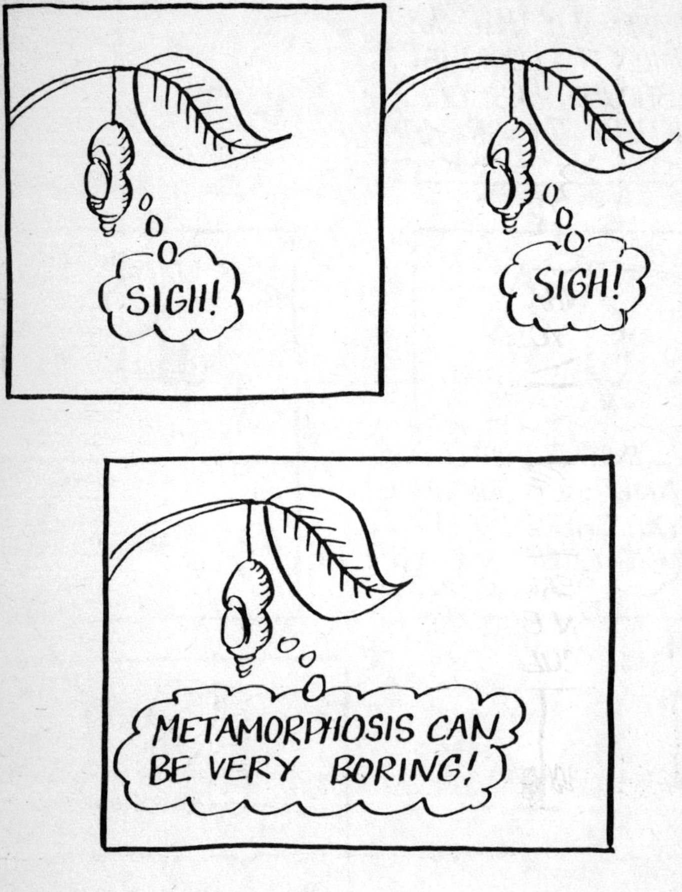
SIGH!
SIGH!
METAMORPHOSIS CAN BE VERY BORING!

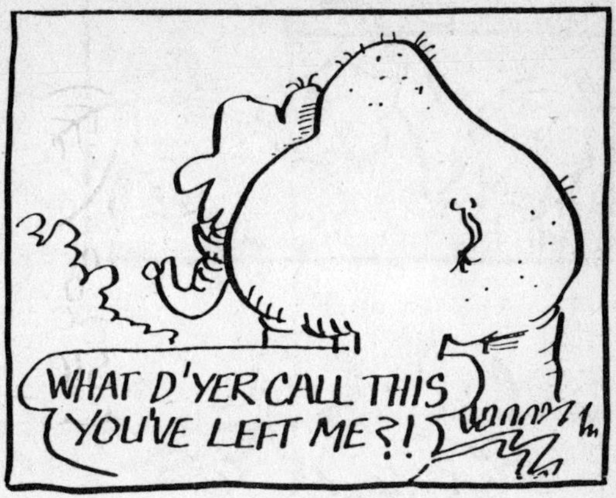
WHAT D'YER CALL THIS YOU'VE LEFT ME?!

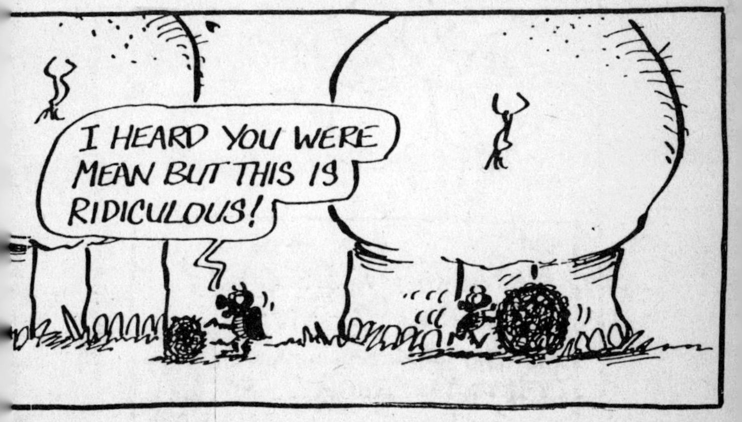
I HEARD YOU WERE MEAN BUT THIS IS RIDICULOUS!

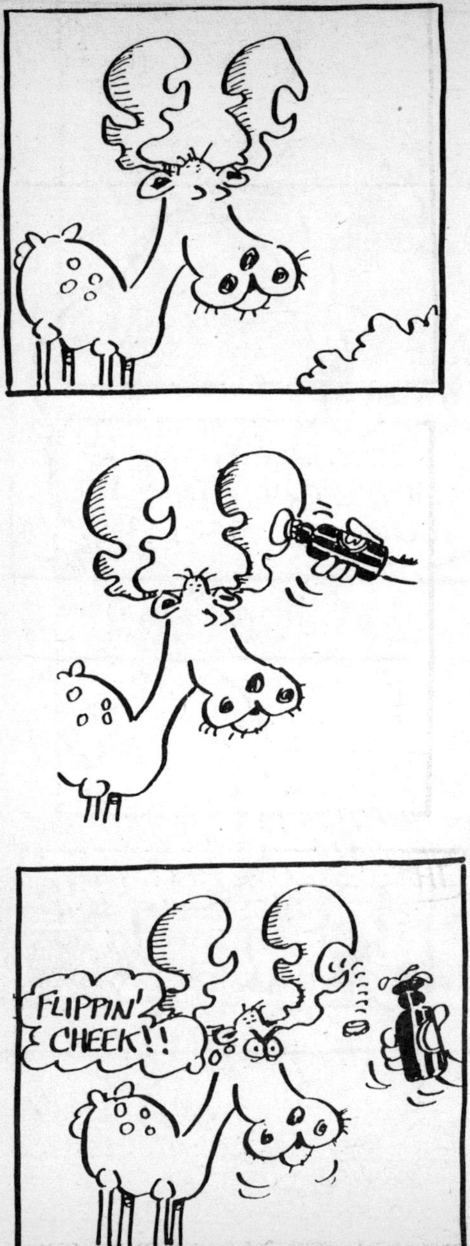
FLIPPIN' CHEEK!!

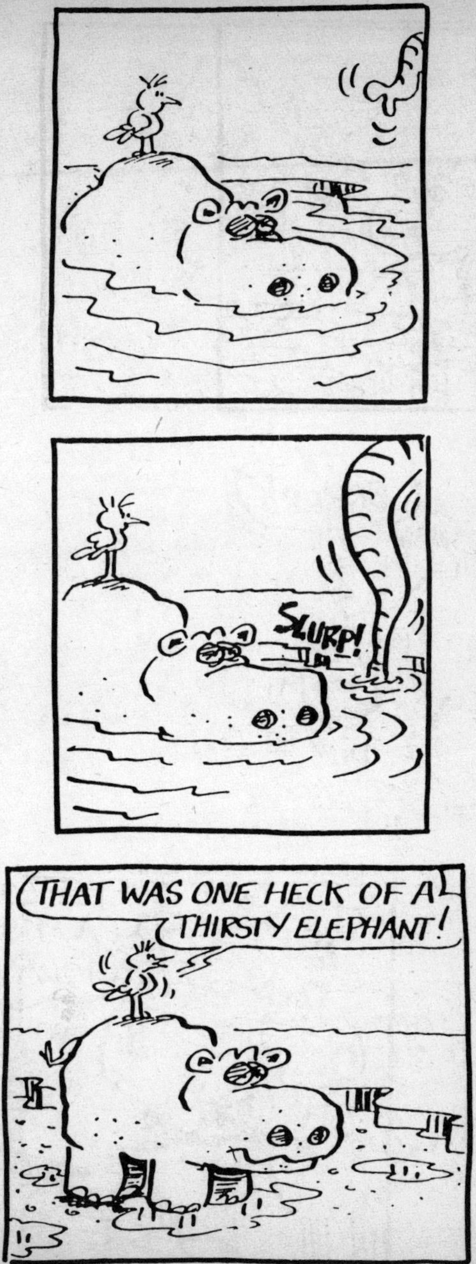
SLURP!
THAT WAS ONE HECK OF A THIRSTY ELEPHANT!

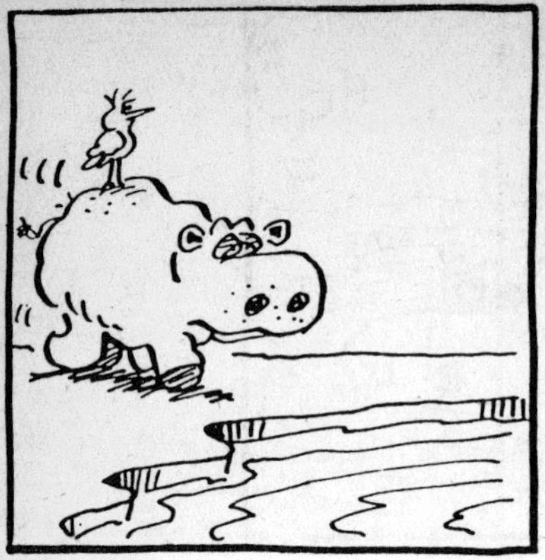

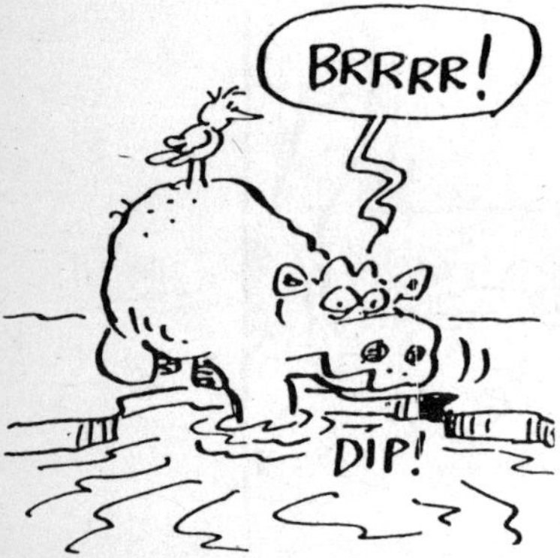
BRRRR!
DIP!

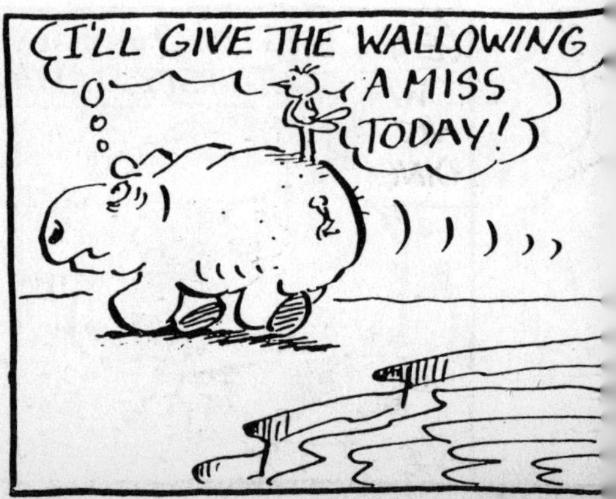
I'LL GIVE THE WALLOWING A MISS TODAY!

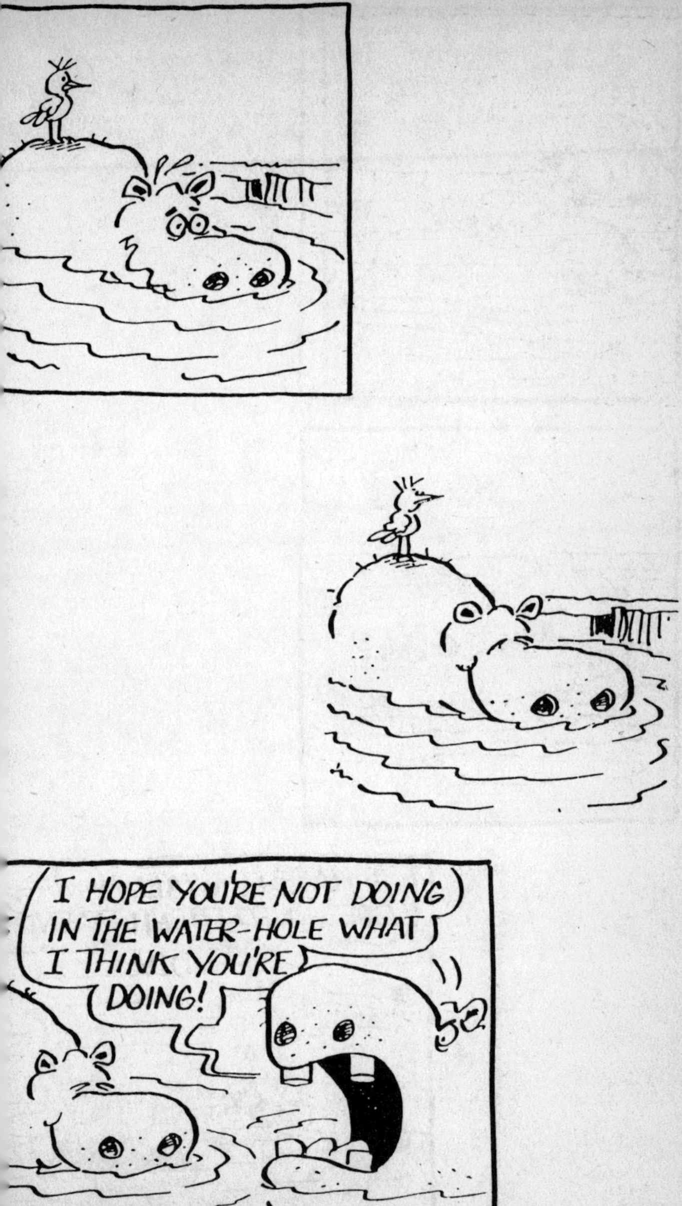
I HOPE YOU'RE NOT DOING IN THE WATER-HOLE WHAT I THINK YOU'RE DOING!

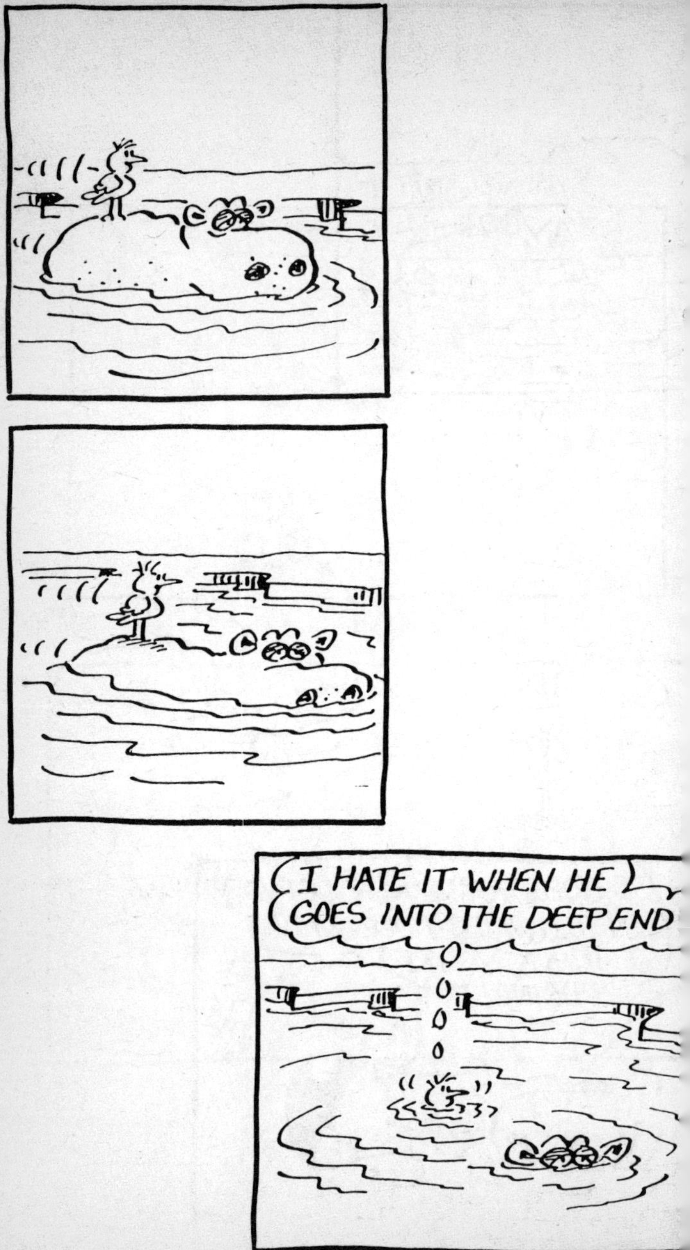
I HATE IT WHEN HE GOES INTO THE DEEP END

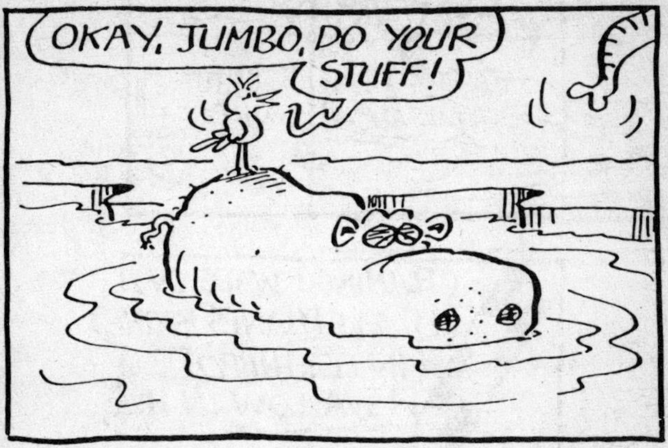
OKAY, JUMBO, DO YOUR STUFF!

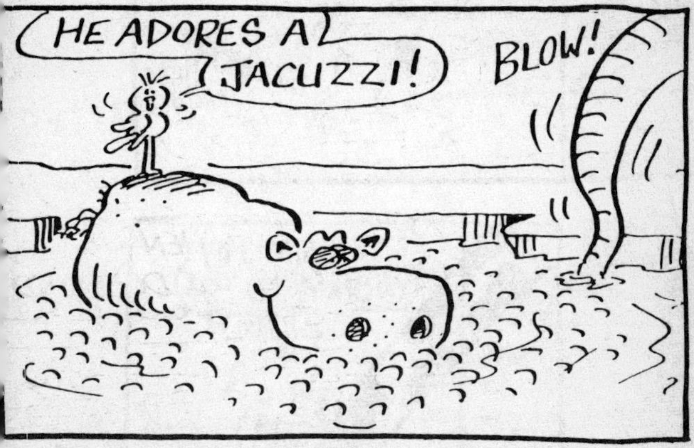
HE ADORES A JACUZZI!
BLOW!

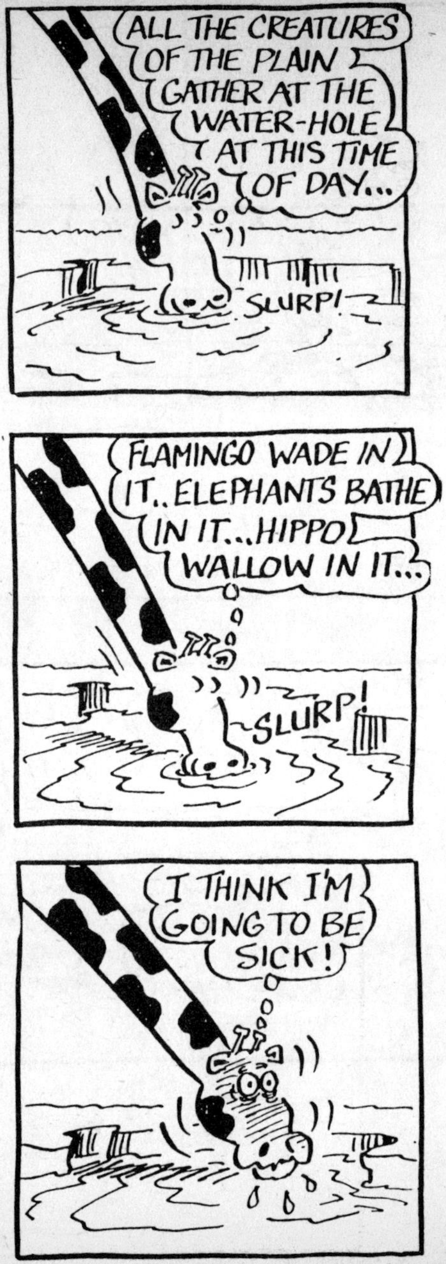
ALL THE CREATURES OF THE PLAIN GATHER AT THE WATER-HOLE AT THIS TIME OF DAY...
SLURP!
FLAMINGO WADE IN IT.. ELEPHANTS BATHE IN IT...HIPPO WALLOW IN IT...
SLURP!
I THINK I'M GOING TO BE SICK!

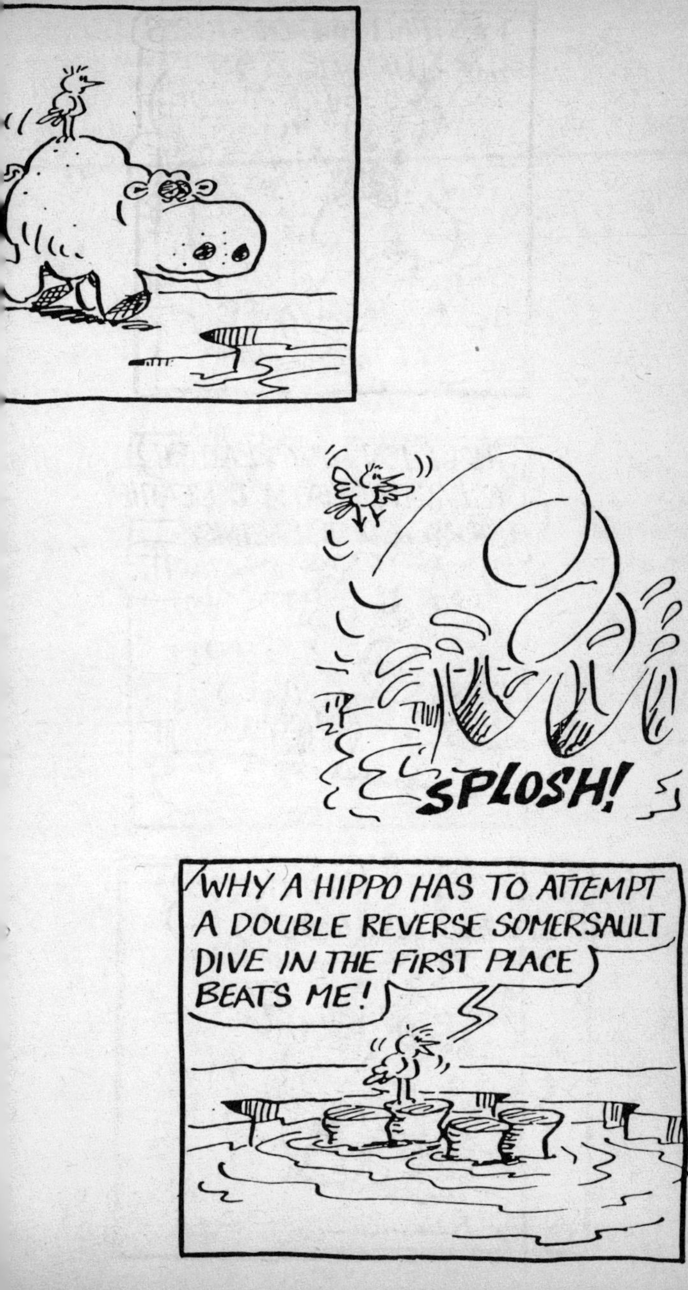
SPLOSH!
WHY A HIPPO HAS TO ATTEMPT A DOUBLE REVERSE SOMERSAULT DIVE IN THE FIRST PLACE BEATS ME!

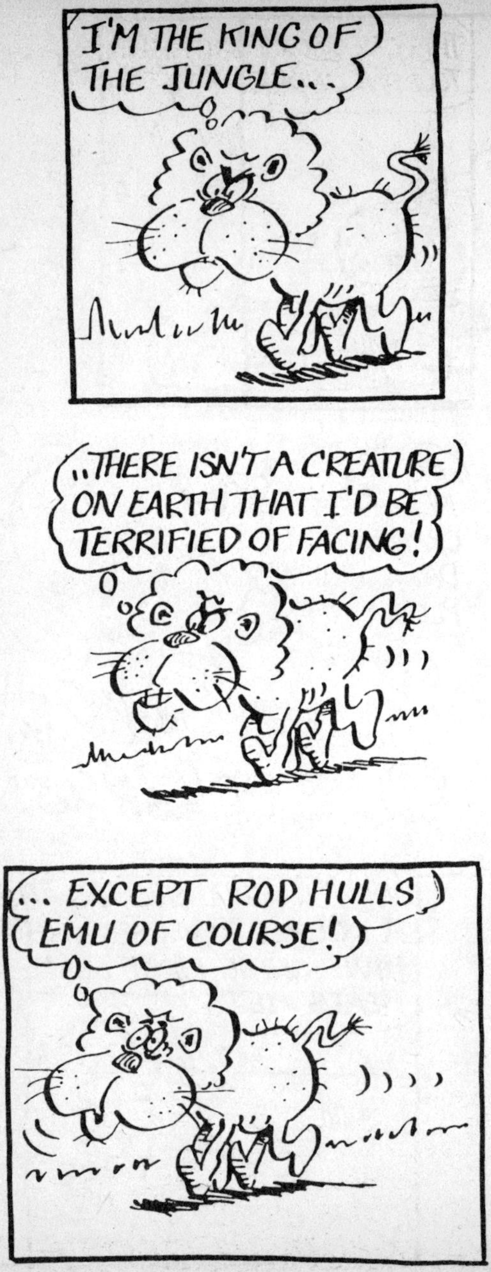
I'M THE KING OF THE JUNGLE...
..THERE ISN'T A CREATURE ON EARTH THAT I'D BE TERRIFIED OF FACING!
... EXCEPT ROD HULLS EMU OF COURSE!

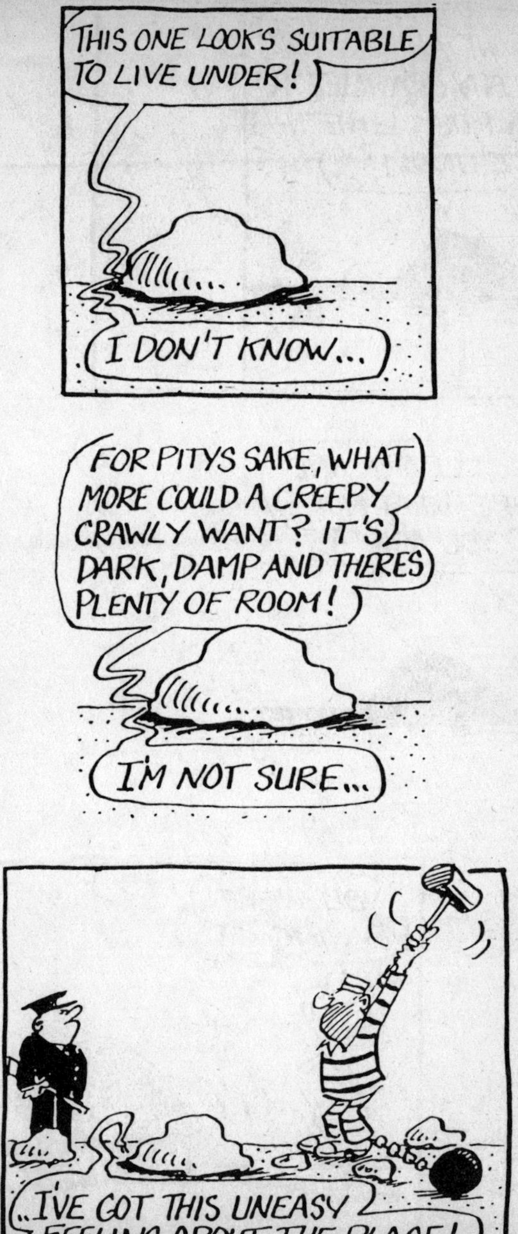
THIS ONE LOOKS SUITABLE TO LIVE UNDER!
I DON'T KNOW...
FOR PITYS SAKE, WHAT MORE COULD A CREEPY CRAWLY WANT? IT'S DARK, DAMP AND THERES PLENTY OF ROOM!
I'M NOT SURE...
..I'VE GOT THIS UNEASY FEELING ABOUT THE PLACE!

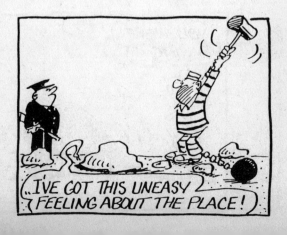

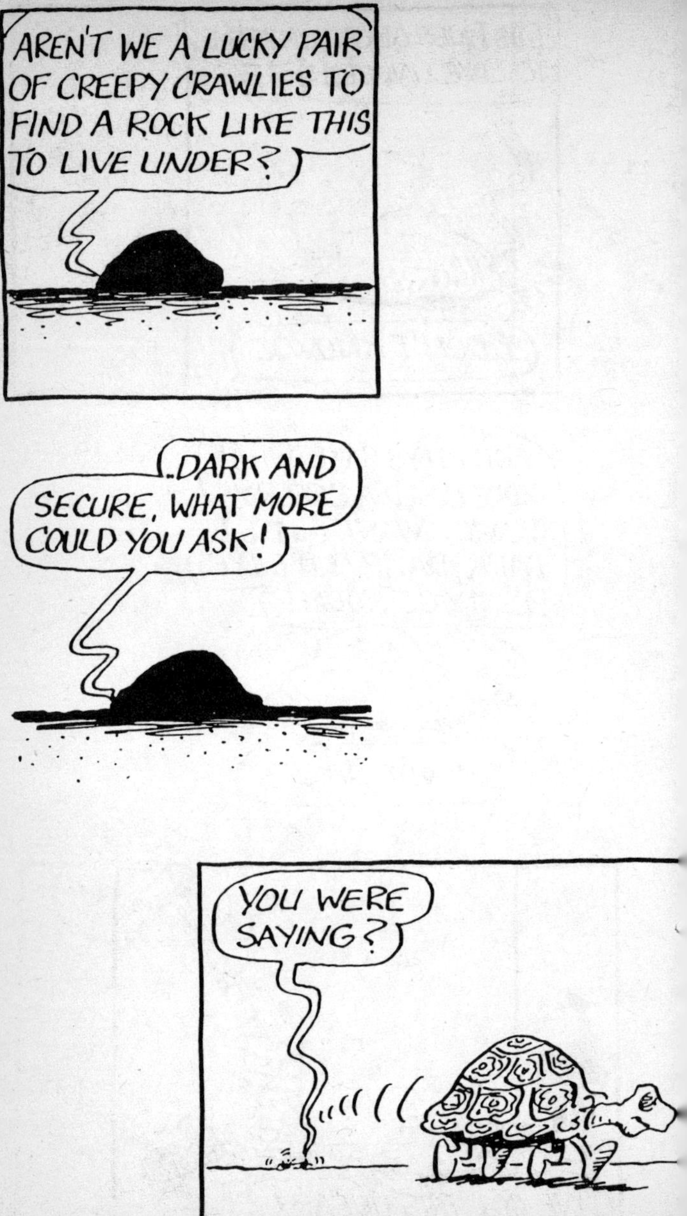
AREN'T WE A LUCKY PAIR OF CREEPY CRAWLIES TO FIND A ROCK LIKE THIS TO LIVE UNDER?
..DARK AND SECURE, WHAT MORE COULD YOU ASK!
YOU WERE SAYING?

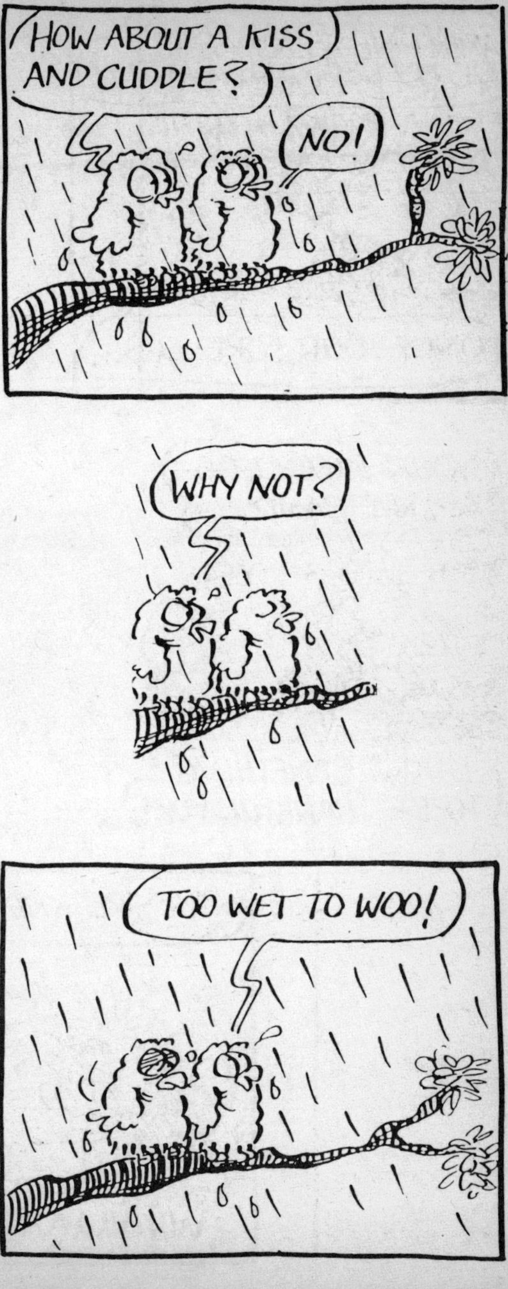
HOW ABOUT A KISS AND CUDDLE?
NO!
WHY NOT?
TOO WET TO WOO!

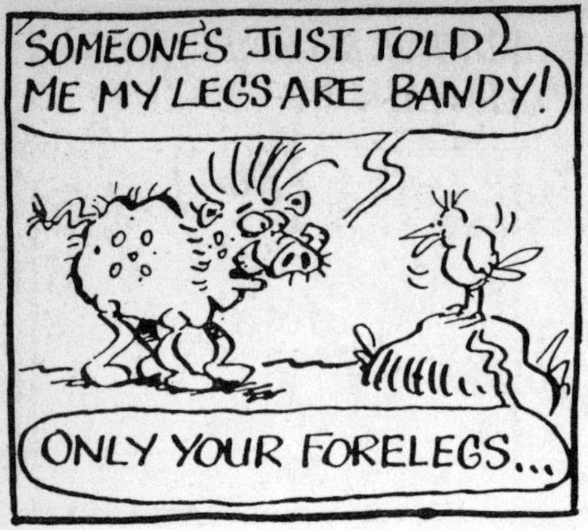
SOMEONE'S JUST TOLD ME MY LEGS ARE BANDY!
ONLY YOUR FORELEGS...

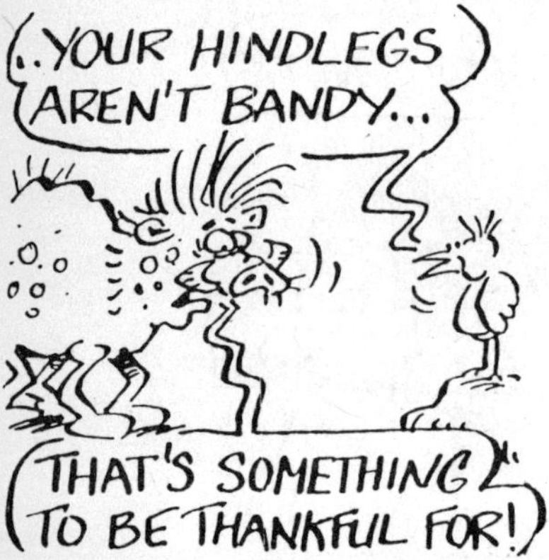
..YOUR HINDLEGS AREN'T BANDY...
THAT'S SOMETHING TO BE THANKFUL FOR!

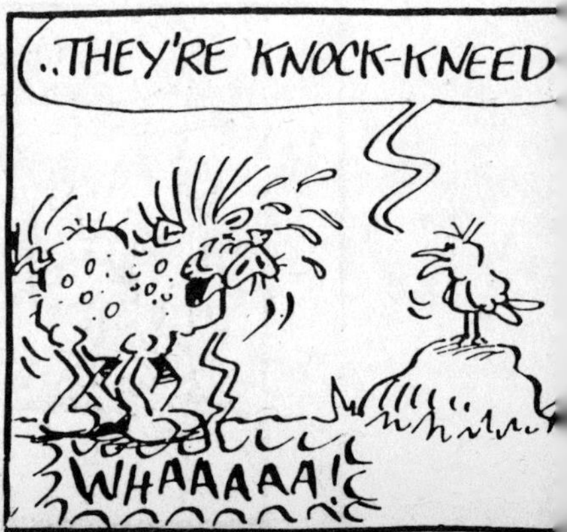
..THEY'RE KNOCK-KNEED
WHAAAAA!

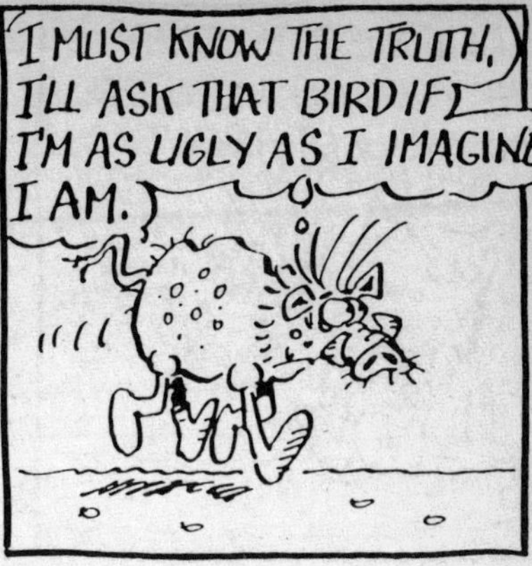
I MUST KNOW THE TRUTH, I'LL ASK THAT BIRD IF I'M AS UGLY AS I IMAGINE I AM.

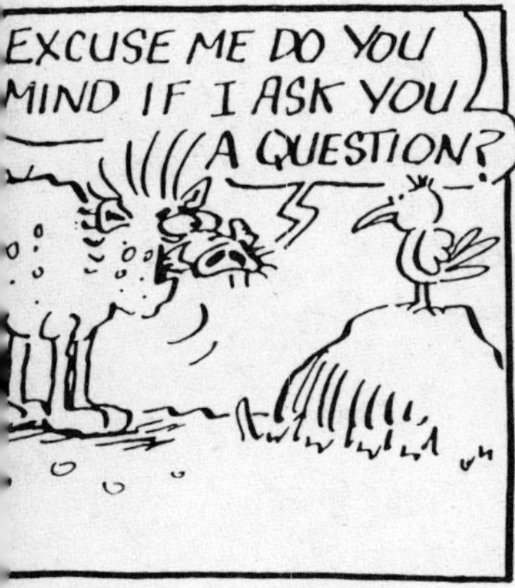
EXCUSE ME DO YOU MIND IF I ASK YOU A QUESTION?

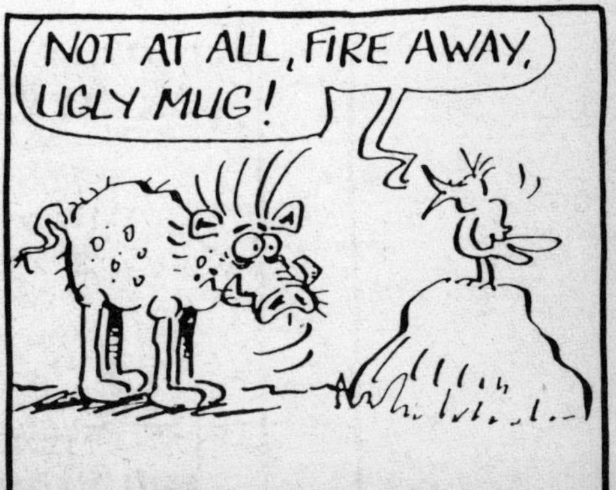
NOT AT ALL, FIRE AWAY, UGLY MUG!

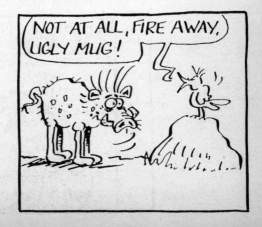

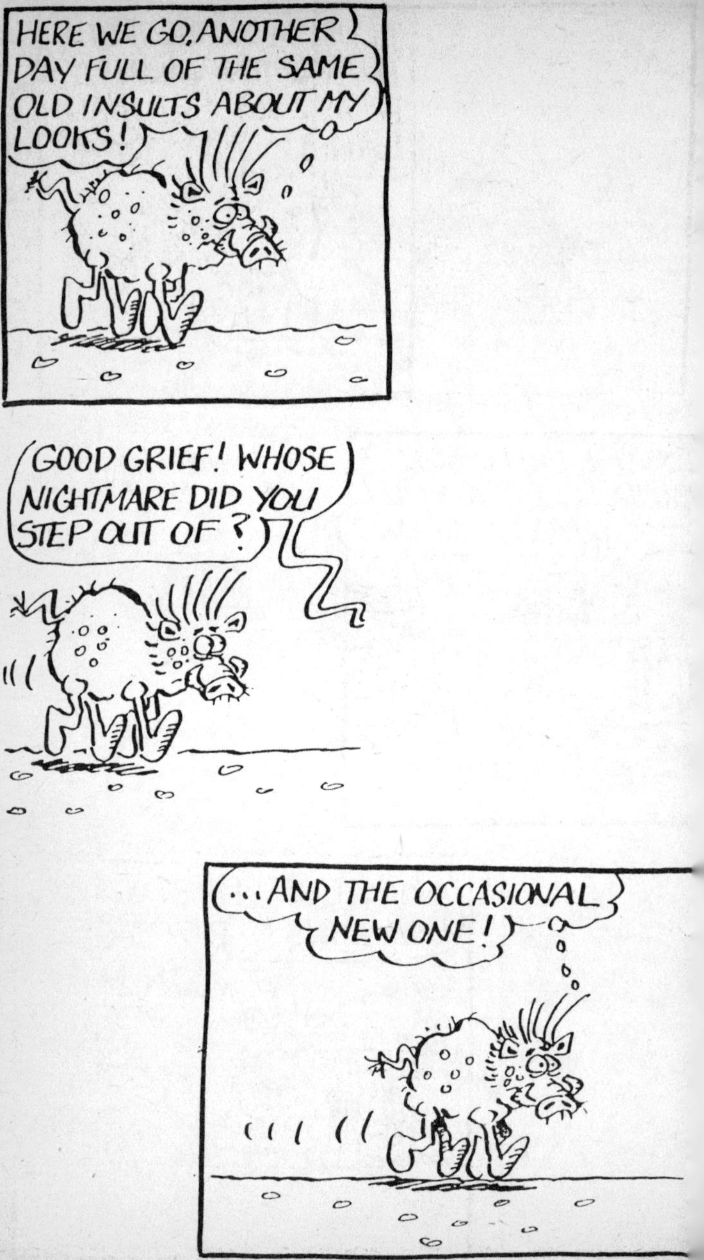
HERE WE GO, ANOTHER DAY FULL OF THE SAME OLD INSULTS ABOUT MY LOOKS!
GOOD GRIEF! WHOSE NIGHTMARE DID YOU STEP OUT OF?
...AND THE OCCASIONAL NEW ONE!

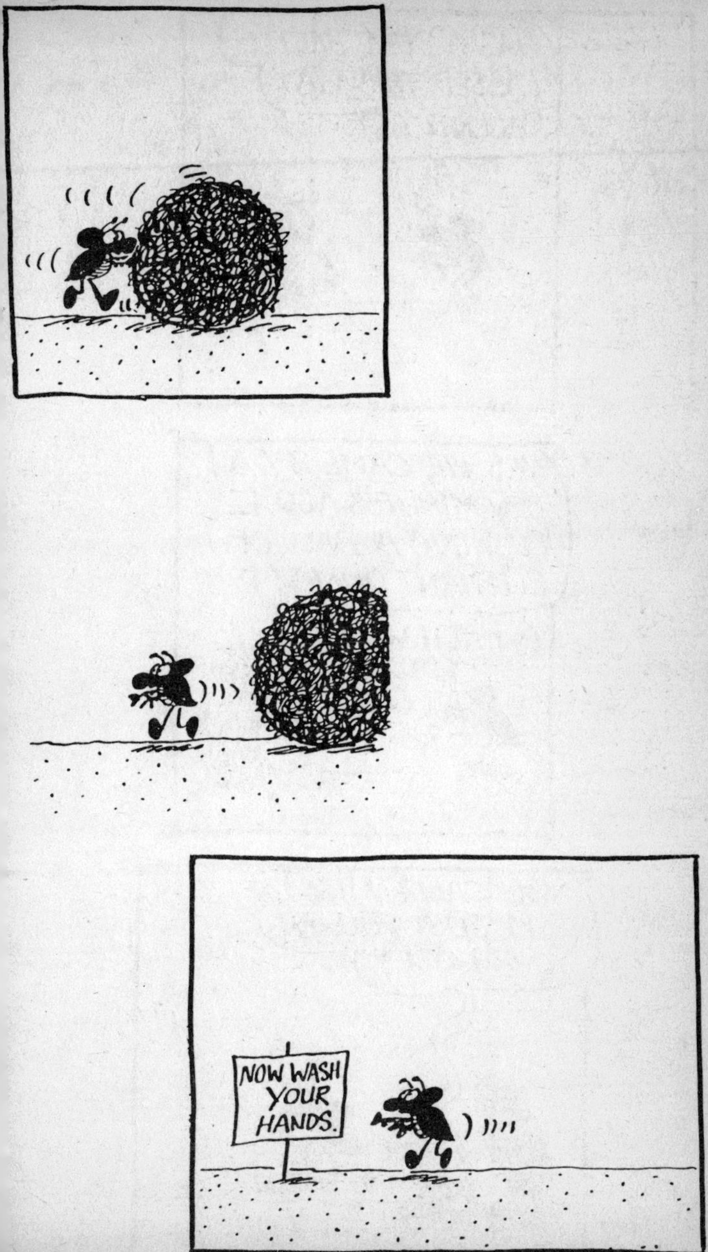
NOW WASH YOUR HANDS.

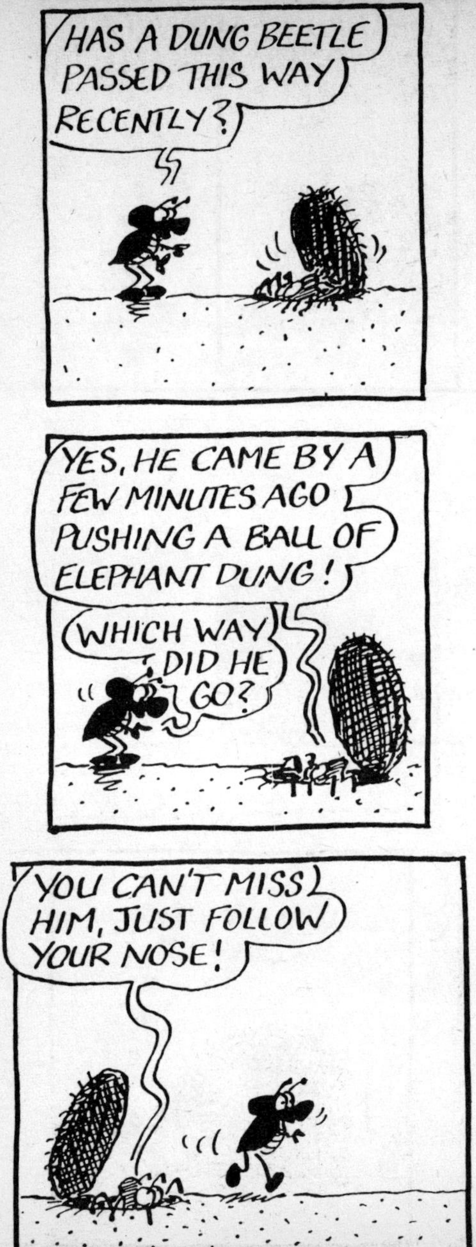
HAS A DUNG BEETLE PASSED THIS WAY RECENTLY?
YES, HE CAME BY A FEW MINUTES AGO PUSHING A BALL OF ELEPHANT DUNG!
WHICH WAY DID HE GO?
YOU CAN'T MISS HIM, JUST FOLLOW YOUR NOSE!

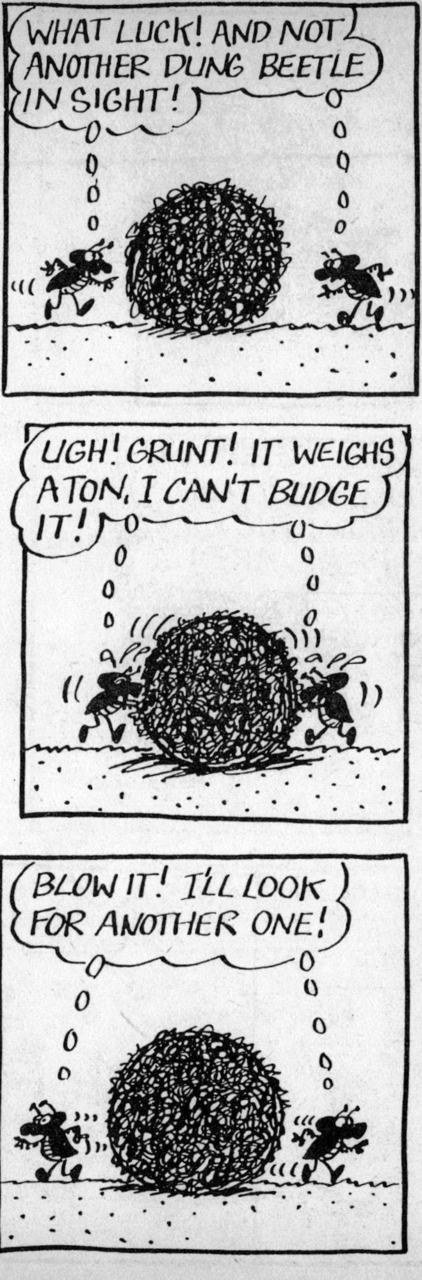
WHAT LUCK! AND NOT ANOTHER DUNG BEETLE IN SIGHT!
UGH! GRUNT! IT WEIGHS A TON. I CAN'T BUDGE IT!
BLOW IT! I'LL LOOK FOR ANOTHER ONE!

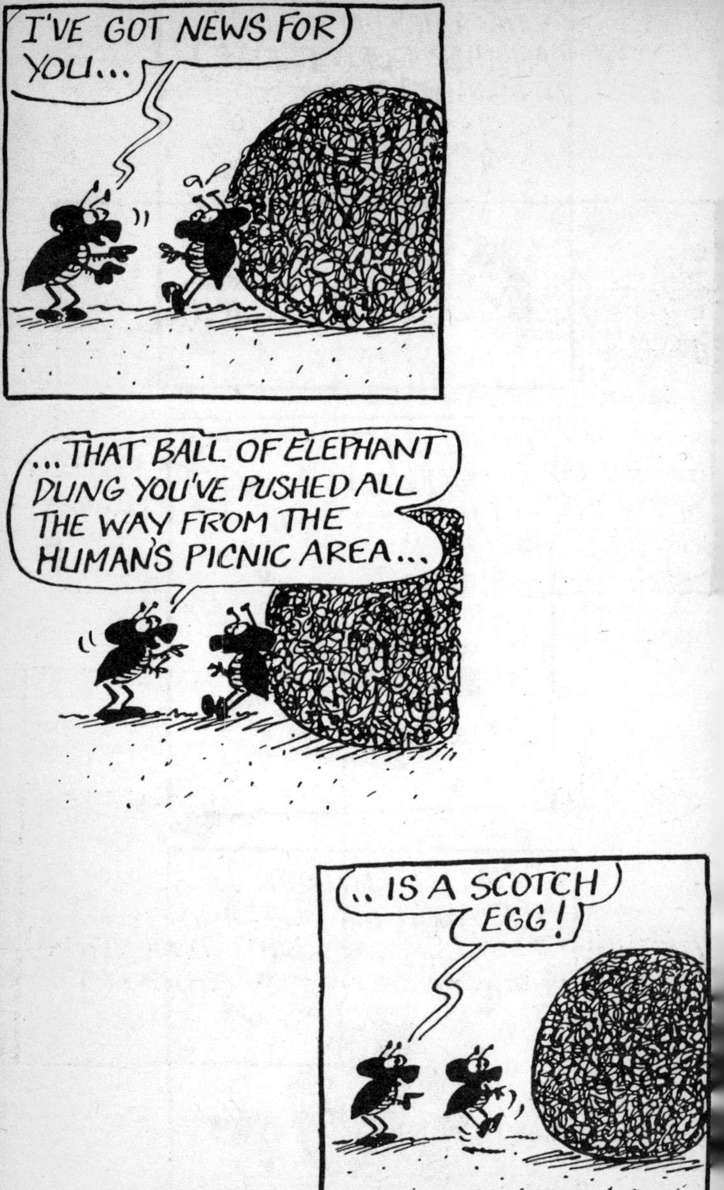
I'VE GOT NEWS FOR YOU...
...THAT BALL OF ELEPHANT DUNG YOU'VE PUSHED ALL THE WAY FROM THE HUMAN'S PICNIC AREA...
.. IS A SCOTCH EGG!

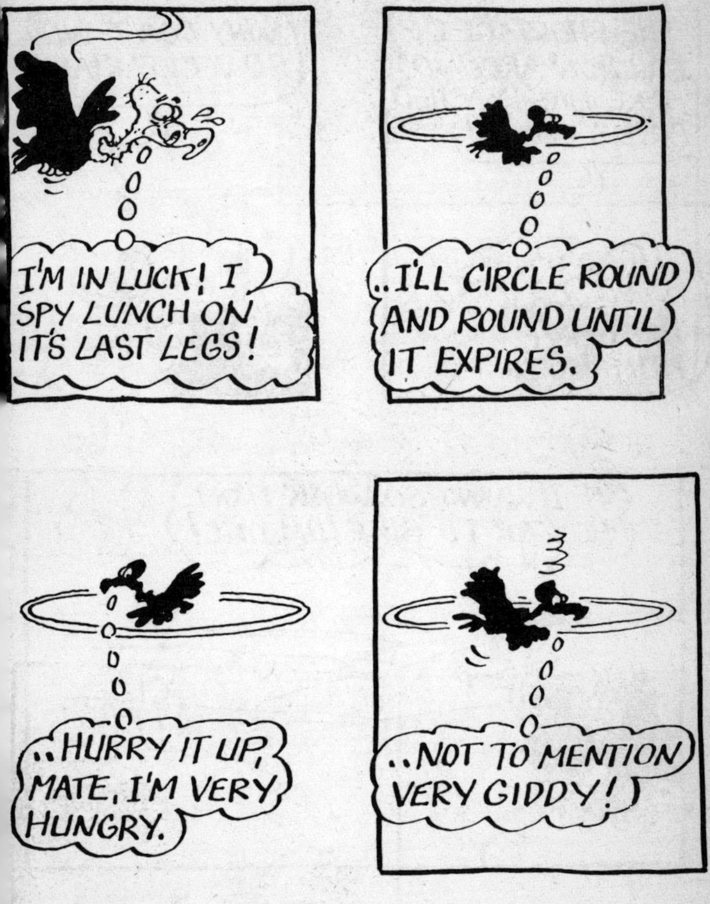
I'M IN LUCK! I SPY LUNCH ON IT'S LAST LEGS!
..I'LL CIRCLE ROUND AND ROUND UNTIL IT EXPIRES.
..HURRY IT UP, MATE, I'M VERY HUNGRY.
..NOT TO MENTION VERY GIDDY!

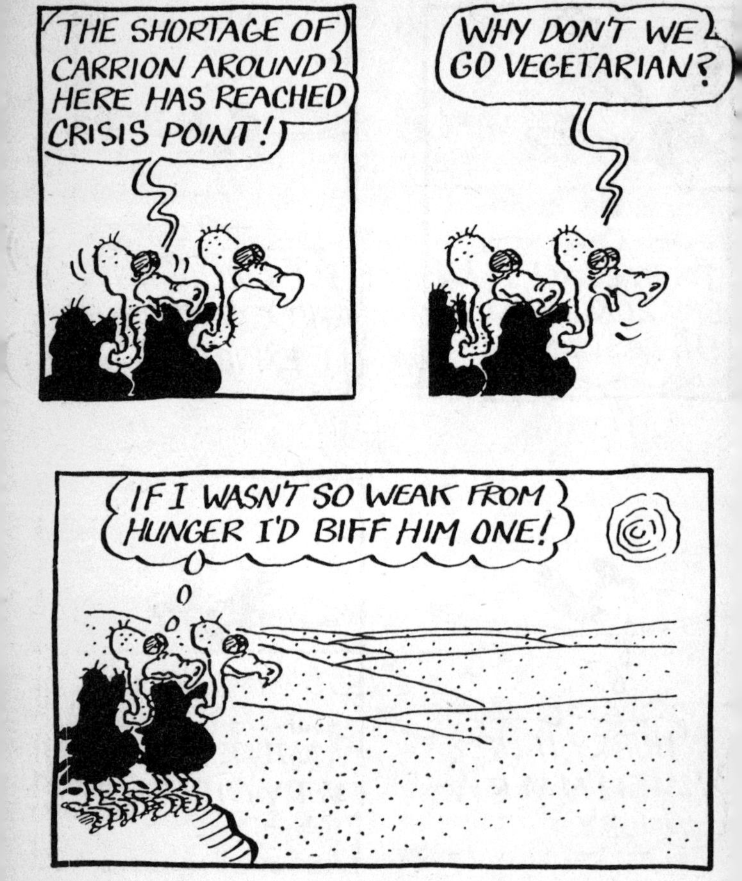
THE SHORTAGE OF CARRION AROUND HERE HAS REACHED CRISIS POINT!
WHY DON'T WE GO VEGETARIAN?
IF I WASN'T SO WEAK FROM HUNGER I'D BIFF HIM ONE!

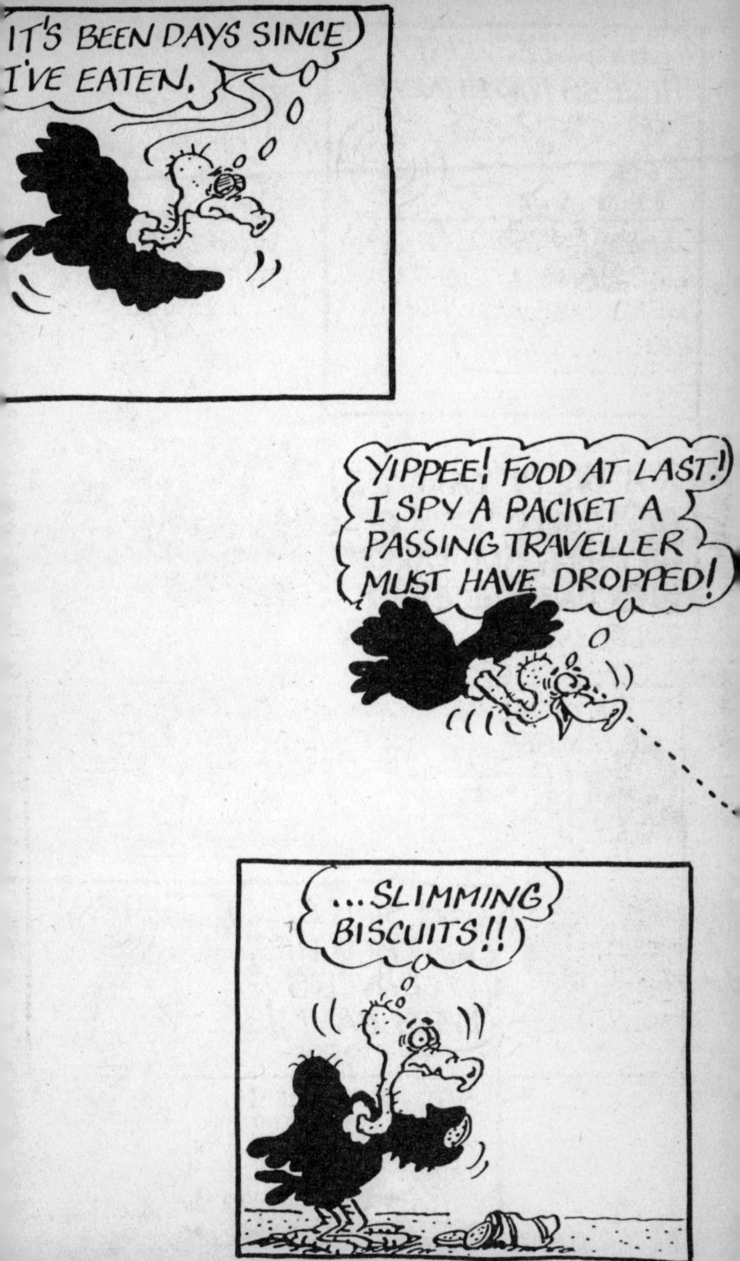
IT'S BEEN DAYS SINCE I'VE EATEN.
YIPPEE! FOOD AT LAST! I SPY A PACKET A PASSING TRAVELLER MUST HAVE DROPPED!
...SLIMMING BISCUITS!!

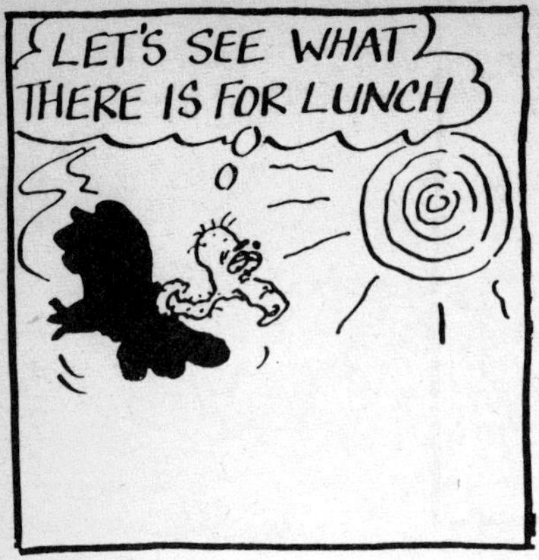
LET'S SEE WHAT THERE IS FOR LUNCH

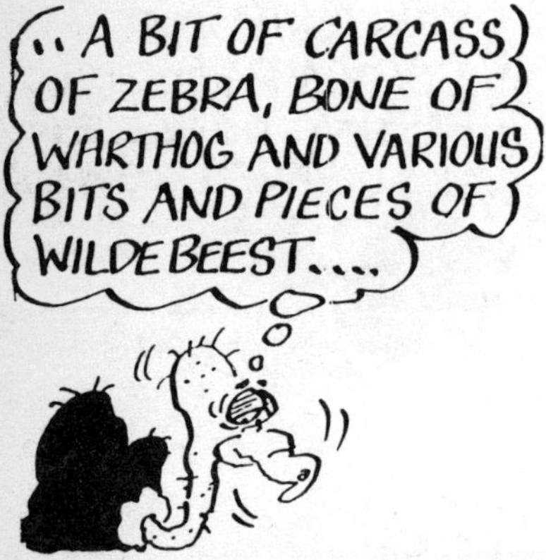
.. A BIT OF CARCASS OF ZEBRA, BONE OF WARTHOG AND VARIOUS BITS AND PIECES OF WILDEBEEST....

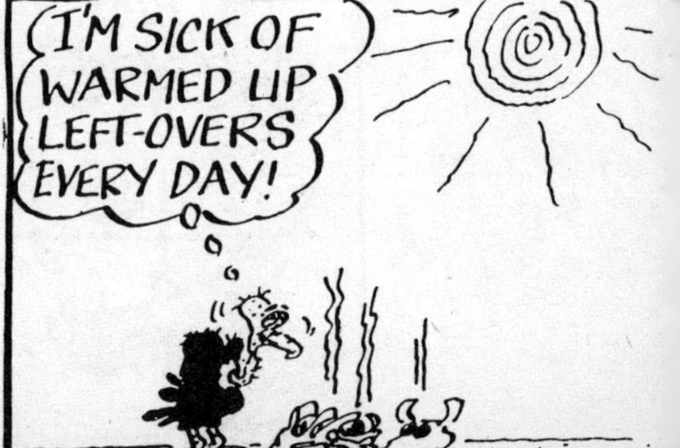
I'M SICK OF WARMED UP LEFT-OVERS EVERY DAY!

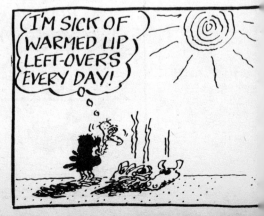

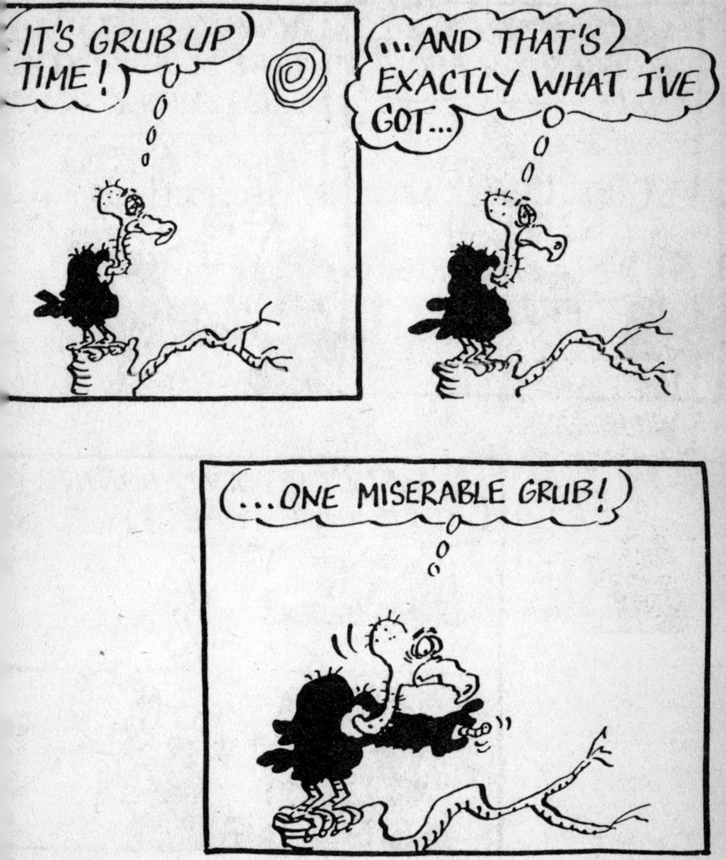
IT'S GRUB UP TIME!
...AND THAT'S EXACTLY WHAT I'VE GOT...
...ONE MISERABLE GRUB!

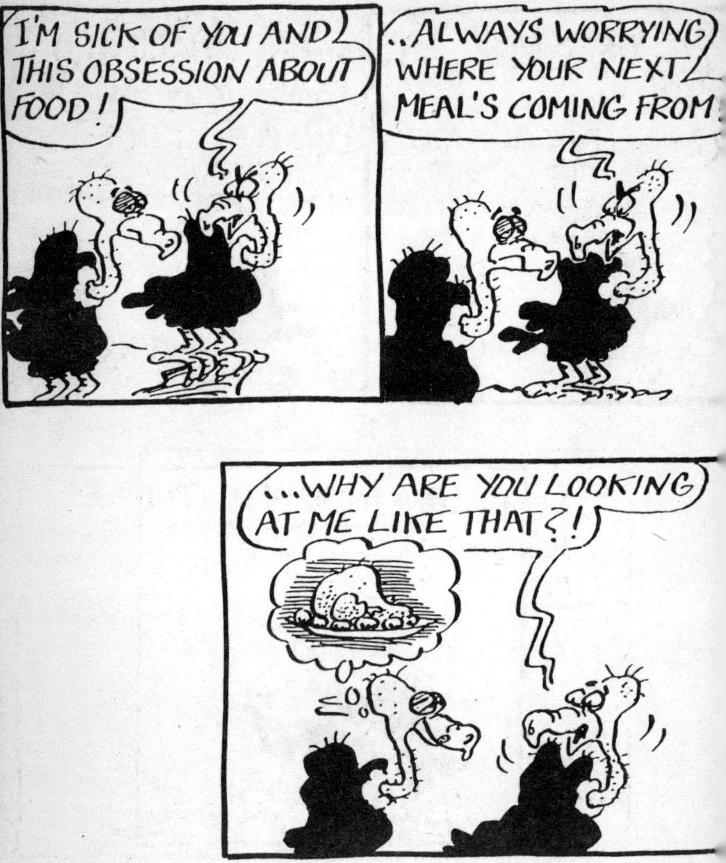
I'M SICK OF YOU AND THIS OBSESSION ABOUT FOOD!
..ALWAYS WORRYING WHERE YOUR NEXT MEAL'S COMING FROM!
...WHY ARE YOU LOOKING AT ME LIKE THAT?!

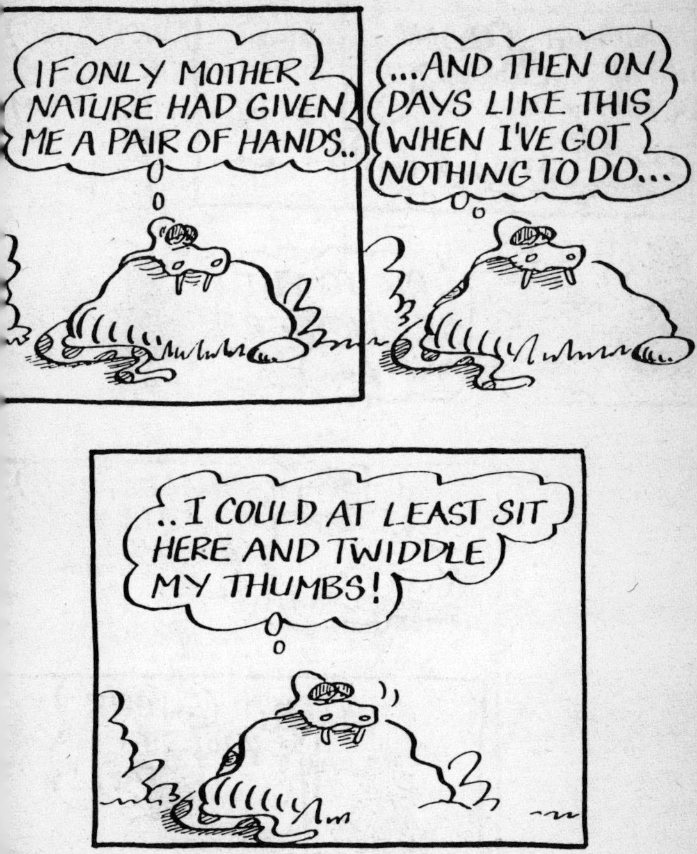
IF ONLY MOTHER NATURE HAD GIVEN ME A PAIR OF HANDS..
...AND THEN ON DAYS LIKE THIS WHEN I'VE GOT NOTHING TO DO...
..I COULD AT LEAST SIT HERE AND TWIDDLE MY THUMBS!

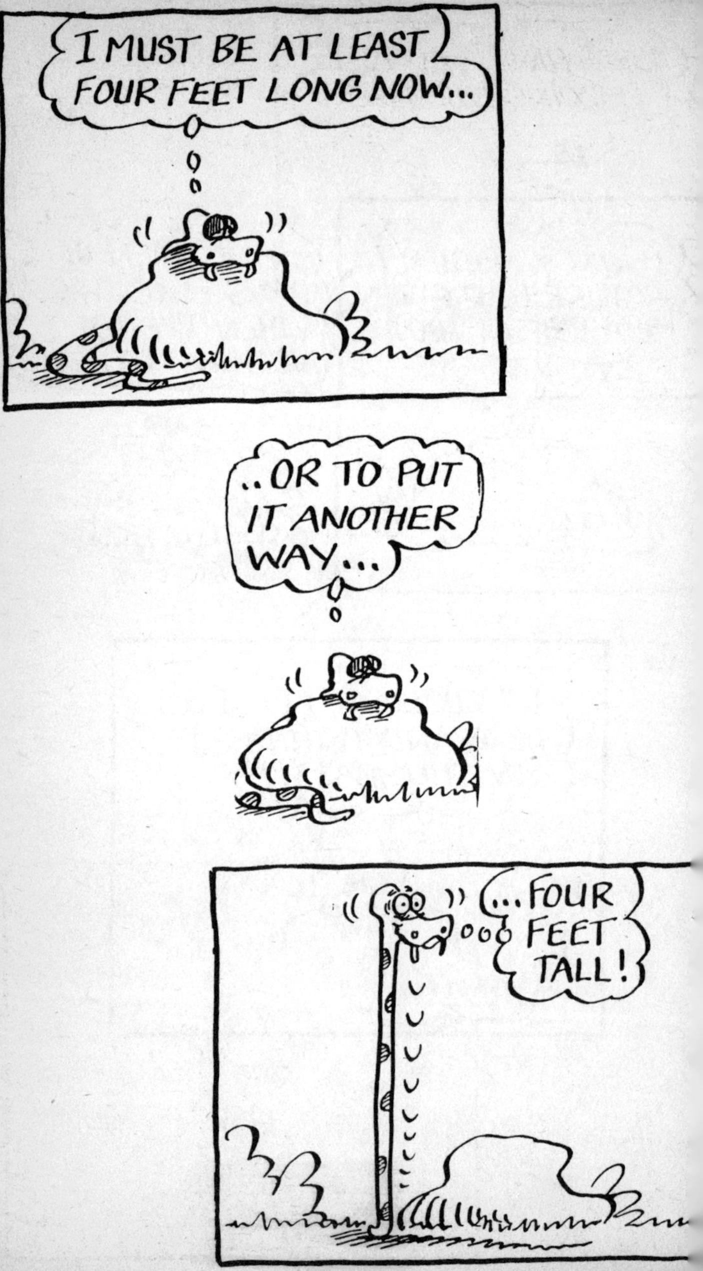
I MUST BE AT LEAST FOUR FEET LONG NOW...
..OR TO PUT IT ANOTHER WAY...
...FOUR FEET TALL!

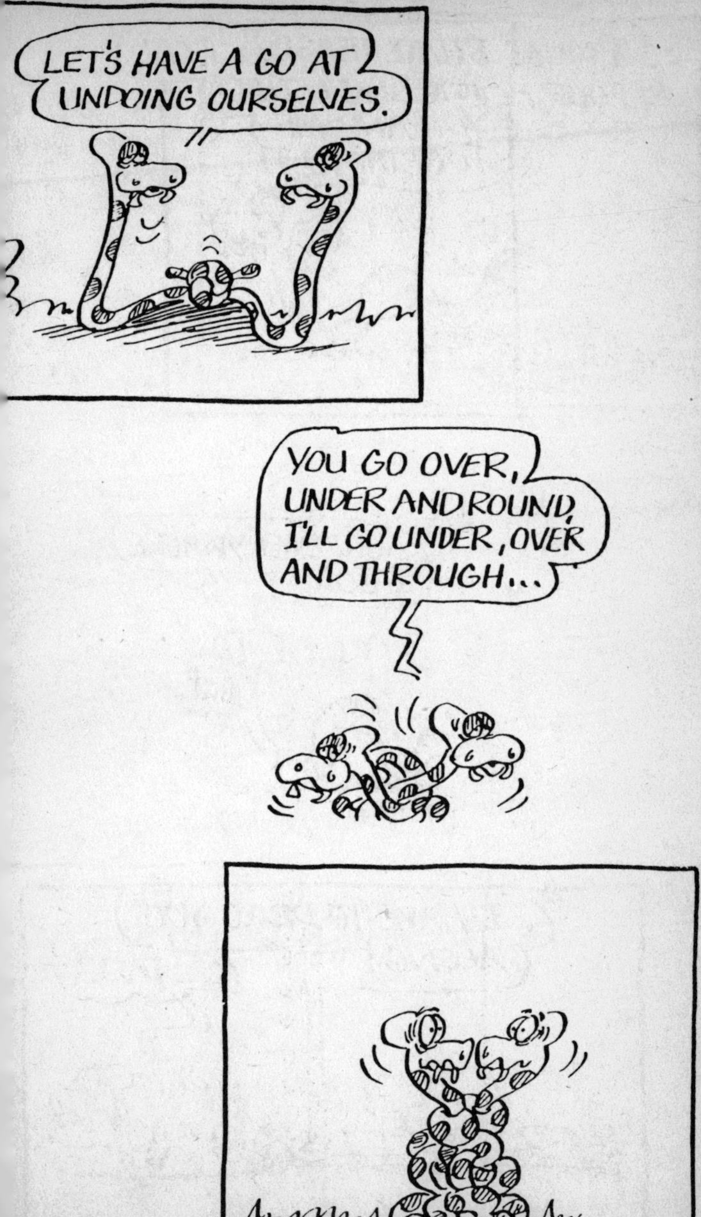
LET'S HAVE A GO AT UNDOING OURSELVES.
YOU GO OVER, UNDER AND ROUND, I'LL GO UNDER, OVER AND THROUGH...

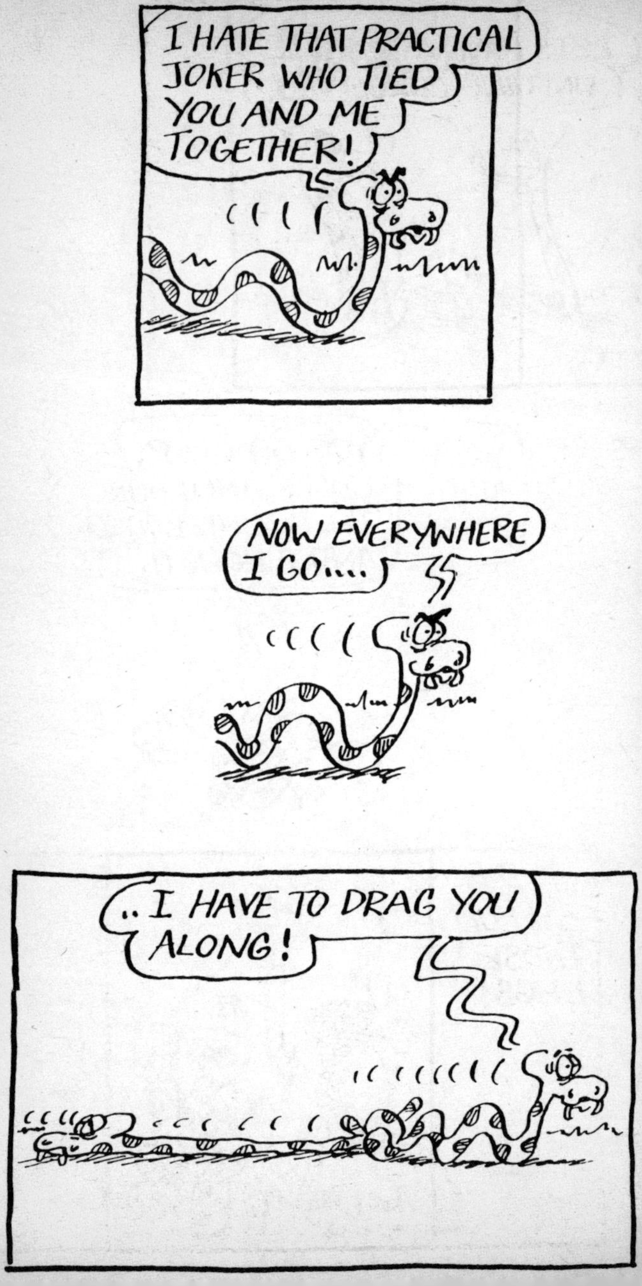
I HATE THAT PRACTICAL JOKER WHO TIED YOU AND ME TOGETHER!
NOW EVERYWHERE I GO....
..I HAVE TO DRAG YOU ALONG!

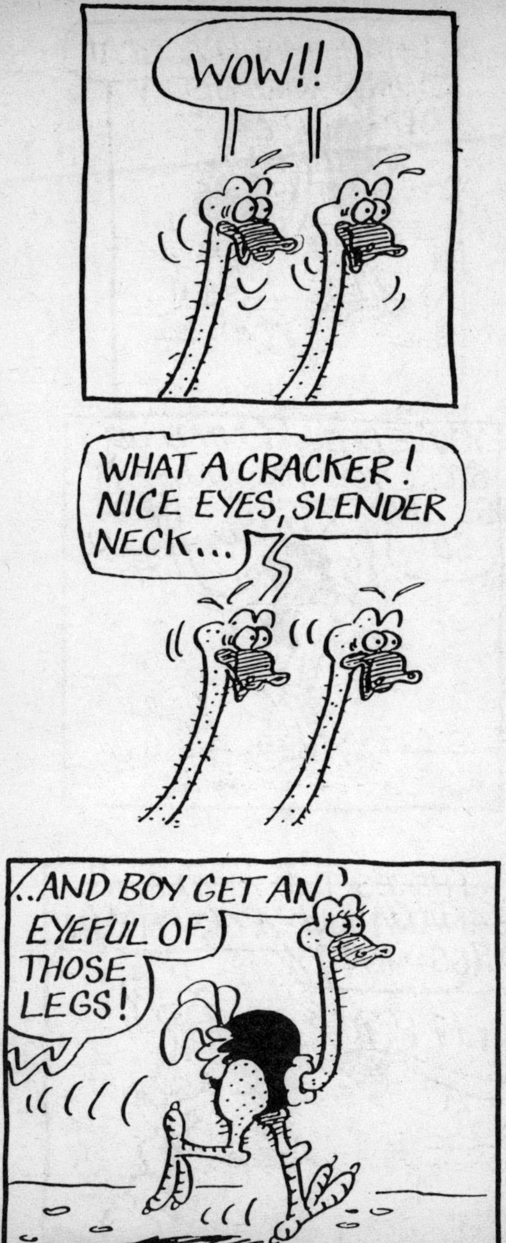
WOW!!
WHAT A CRACKER! NICE EYES, SLENDER NECK...
..AND BOY GET AN EYEFUL OF THOSE LEGS!

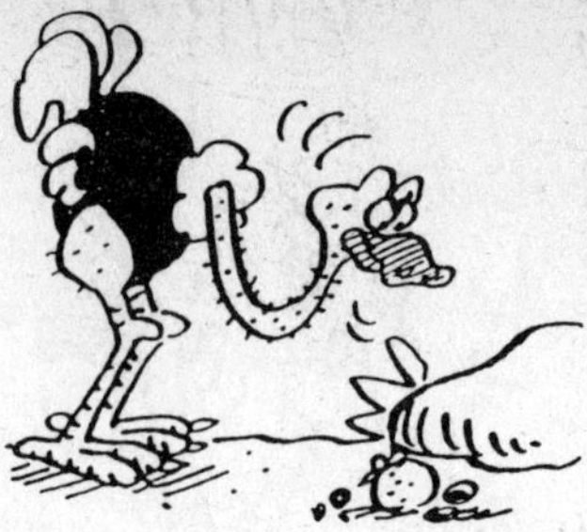

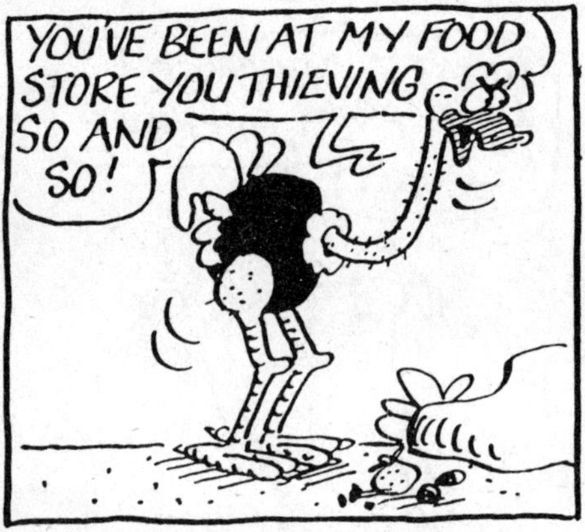
YOU'VE BEEN AT MY FOOD STORE YOU THIEVING SO AND SO!

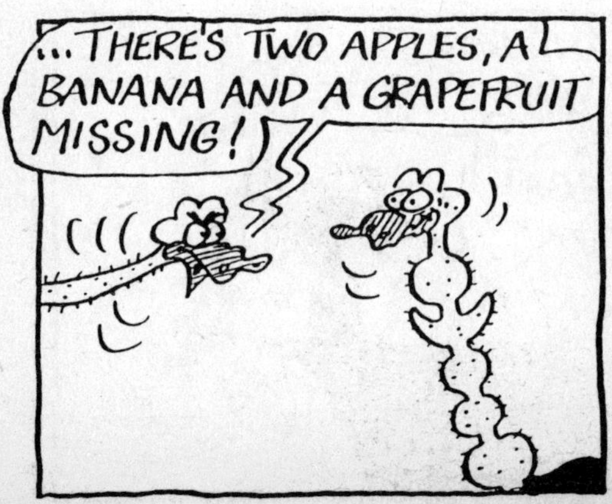
...THERE'S TWO APPLES, A BANANA AND A GRAPEFRUIT MISSING!

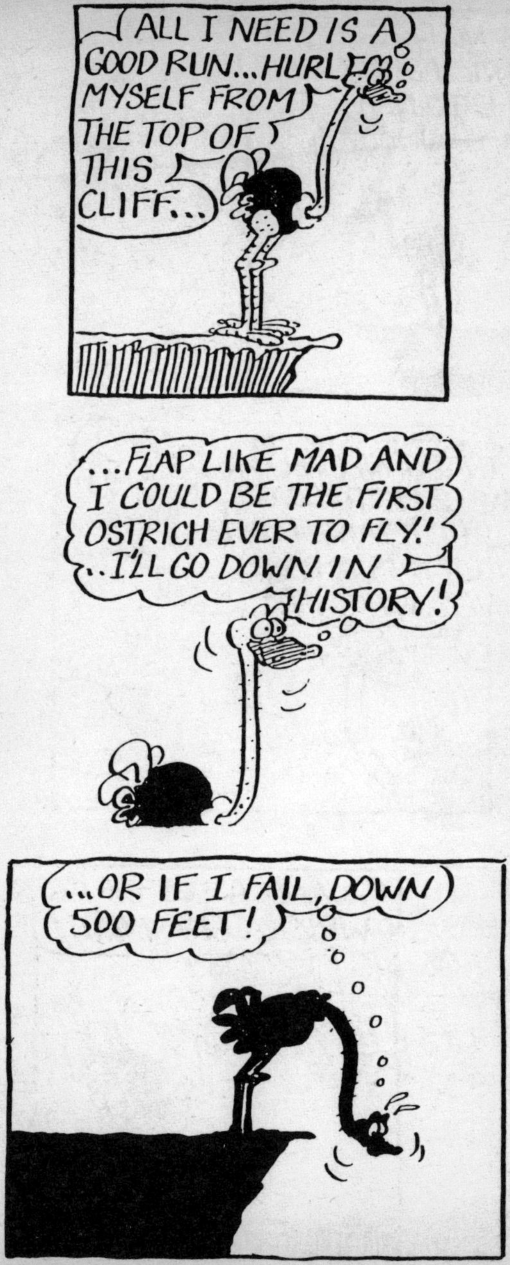

ALL I NEED IS A GOOD RUN... HURL MYSELF FROM THE TOP OF THIS CLIFF...
...FLAP LIKE MAD AND I COULD BE THE FIRST OSTRICH EVER TO FLY! ..I'LL GO DOWN IN HISTORY!
...OR IF I FAIL, DOWN 500 FEET!

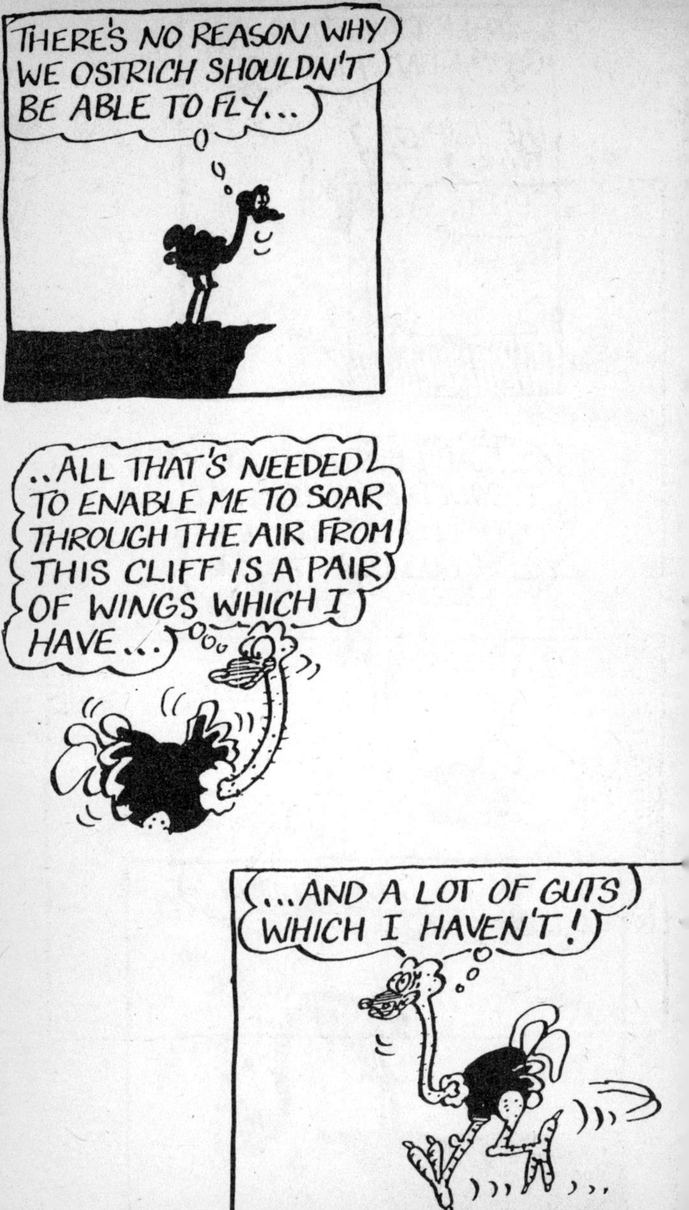
THERE'S NO REASON WHY WE OSTRICH SHOULDN'T BE ABLE TO FLY...
..ALL THAT'S NEEDED TO ENABLE ME TO SOAR THROUGH THE AIR FROM THIS CLIFF IS A PAIR OF WINGS WHICH I HAVE...
...AND A LOT OF GUTS WHICH I HAVEN'T!

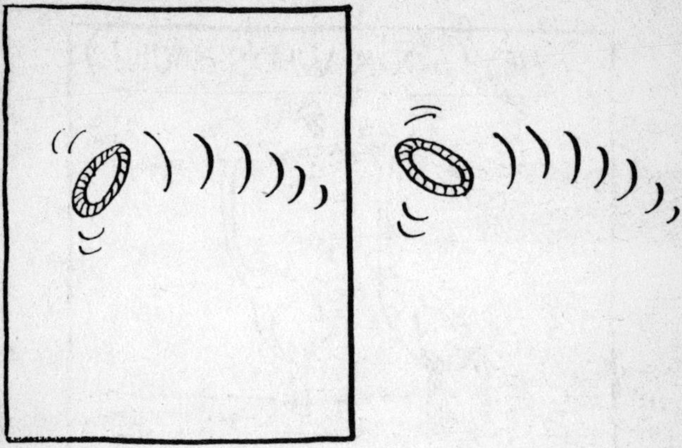

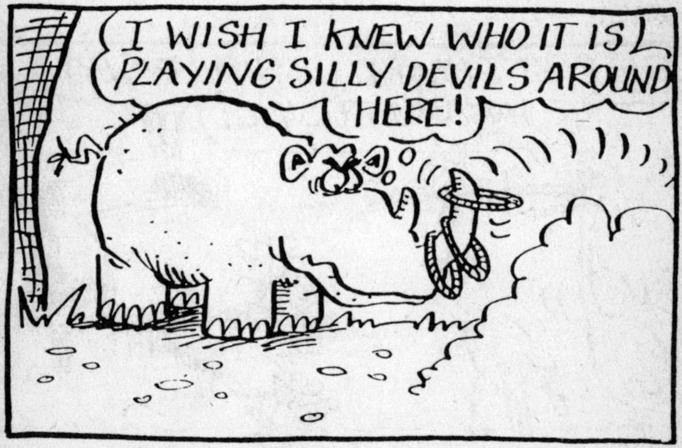
I WISH I KNEW WHO IT IS PLAYING SILLY DEVILS AROUND HERE!

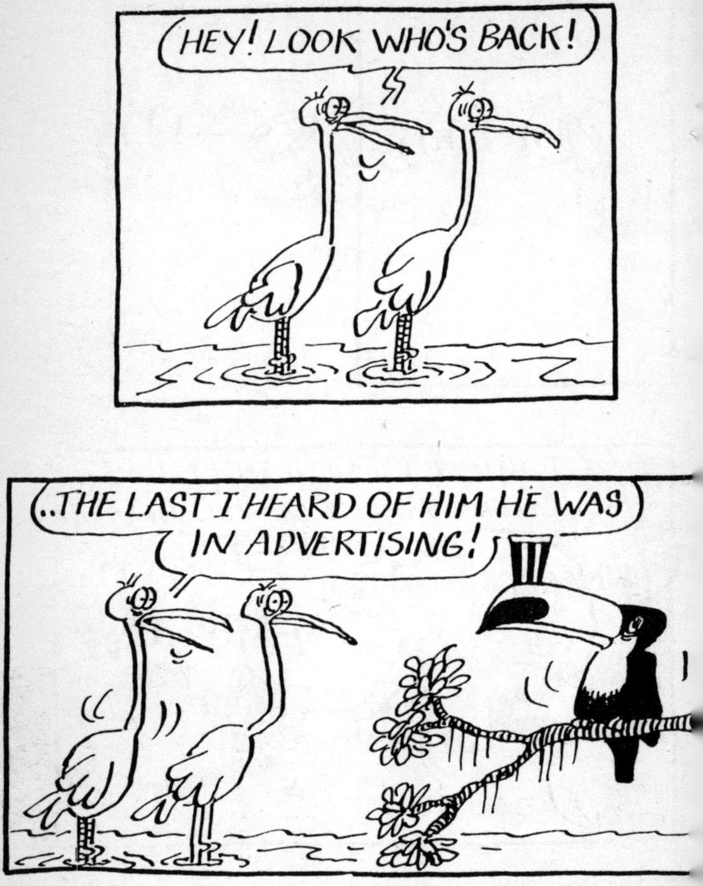
HEY! LOOK WHO'S BACK!
..THE LAST I HEARD OF HIM HE WAS IN ADVERTISING!

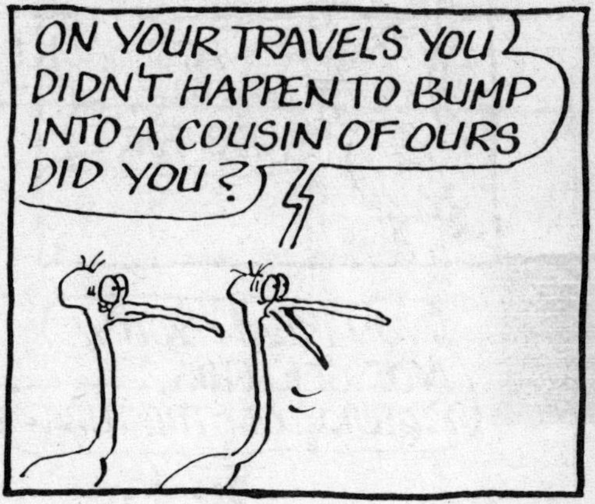
ON YOUR TRAVELS YOU DIDN'T HAPPEN TO BUMP INTO A COUSIN OF OURS DID YOU?

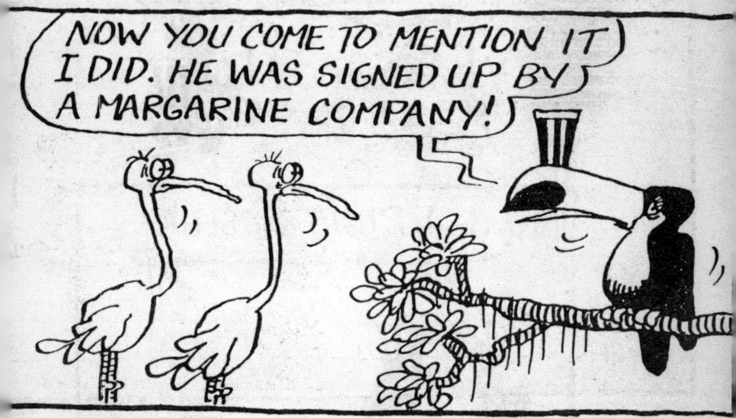
NOW YOU COME TO MENTION IT I DID. HE WAS SIGNED UP BY A MARGARINE COMPANY!

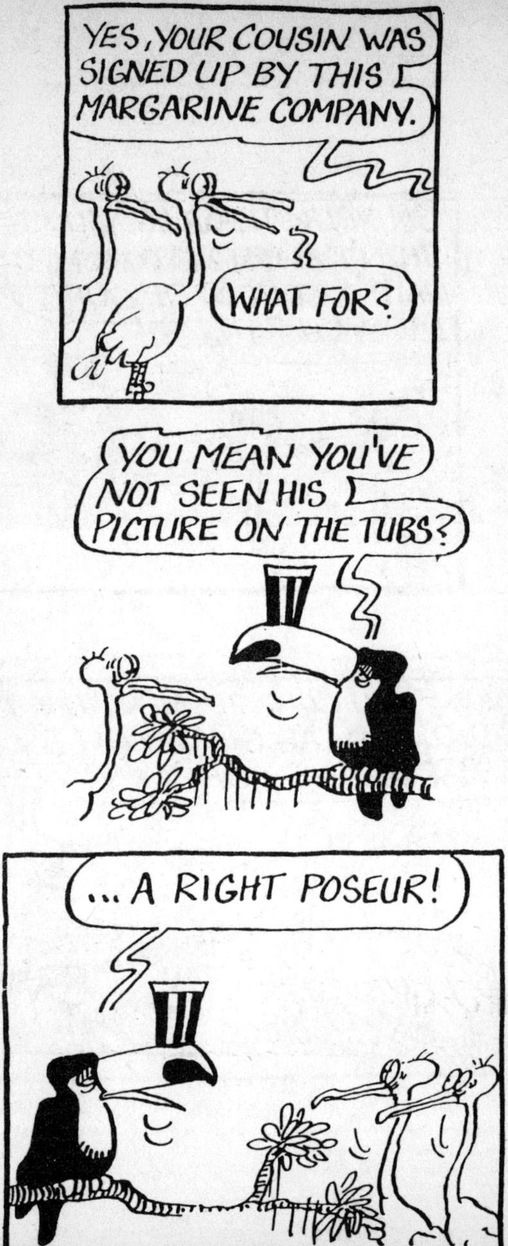
YES, YOUR COUSIN WAS SIGNED UP BY THIS MARGARINE COMPANY.
WHAT FOR?
YOU MEAN YOU'VE NOT SEEN HIS PICTURE ON THE TUBS?
... A RIGHT POSEUR!

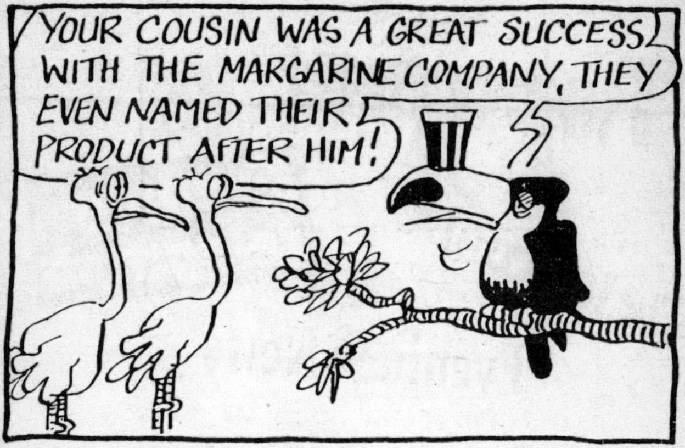
YOUR COUSIN WAS A GREAT SUCCESS! WITH THE MARGARINE COMPANY, THEY EVEN NAMED THEIR PRODUCT AFTER HIM!

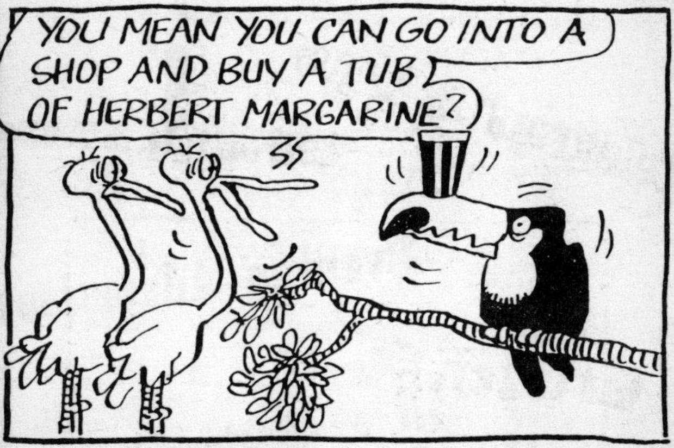
YOU MEAN YOU CAN GO INTO A SHOP AND BUY A TUB OF HERBERT MARGARINE?

CREATURE FEATURE

appears in...

The FUNDAY TIMES

The Journal

Evening Telegraph

Evening News

HULL DAILY Mail

Lincolnshire Echo

Telegraph & Argus

Chronicle & Echo

Evening Advertiser

GLOUCESTERSHIRE Citizen

Eastern Daily Press

Evening News

Western Morning News